MW01243452

To Michael —
Best wishes ---
Enjoy! Ann

It's a LONG WAY
from HALLS

Raymond and Ann Hale

We hope you enjoy reading "It's A Long Way From Halls" as much as Ann and I enjoyed writing it.

Raymond

Ann Hale

Raymond and Ann Hale

It's a
LONG WAY
from HALLS

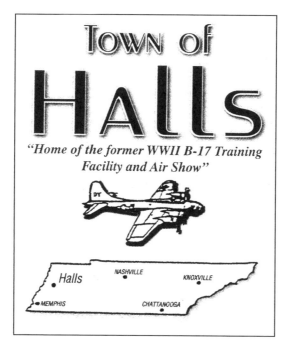

Town of

HALLs

"Home of the former WWII B-17 Training Facility and Air Show"

Halls · NASHVILLE · KNOXVILLE
MEMPHIS · CHATTANOOGA

Raymond & Ann Hale

Waldenhouse Publishers, Inc.
Walden, Tennessee

It's a Long Way from Halls

Printed in the United States of America
Published by Waldenhouse Publishers, Inc.
100 Clegg Street, Signal Mountain, TN 37377 USA
ISBN: 978-1-935186-04-5
Library of Congress Number: 2009925736

HALLS, TENNESSEE
"My Hometown"

HALLS, TENNESSEE, is a small farming community of approximately 2,300 people located in northwest Tennessee, sixty-five miles north of Memphis and thirteen miles south of Dyersburg, just off Highway 51 in Lauderdale County.

Halls was founded in 1812 and named after Hansford R. Hall, one of the founders. The original name was Halls Station. Early business ventures included sawmills, cotton gins and grist mills. The people of Halls depended on agriculture for a living.

Halls experienced its greatest population growth in the 1940's and 1950's. From 1942 to 1945 the Army Air Corps had a B-17 (Flying Fortress) bomber flight training base in Halls, and the growth around the Air Base significantly improved the economy. The influx of people almost doubled the population. In 1945, following World War II, the Air Base closed.

There was less demand for manual laborers in the fields as farm equipment became more sophisticated. In the 1950's many people left the farm lands for employment in northern cities.

The town began to change as the economy declined following the closure of the Air Base and the exodus of farm workers. No longer were the streets bustling with residents, but were desolate and quiet.

In 2008, the people of Halls continue to depend on agriculture for a living. Through the years cotton has been "king" but soy beans are competing with cotton for the number one crop. With the production of alternate fuels to relieve the demand for oil, soy beans are in demand for bio-diesel fuel.

Eateries, shopping and The Veterans' Museum displaying military history are again bringing life to the streets of Halls as there is a rebirth of activity in this sleepy southern town – The Historic Town of Halls.

DEDICATION

This book is dedicated to Ann, my wife, best friend, companion and confidante, who has shared my Christian faith and life's adventures for over fifty-six years.

She has written the text of the book to record the stories told of my life experiences. Ann's commitment to *It's A Long Way From Halls* has made possible the sharing of the journey of a lifetime.

ACKNOWLEDGMENTS

Love and appreciation go to our daughters, Susan Hale Chastain, Joan Hale Bunn, and Dianne Hale Gonzalez, who encouraged me to put into print my life story for my children, grandchildren and others who may find it interesting and entertaining. *It's a Long Way from Halls* is my response to their persuasion to record the "tales and traditions" of my family for future generations.

My love and gratitude go to Ann Ledford Hale, my loving and devoted wife, who has assisted with this book by chronicling the stories so vividly recalled by me. Ann's journalistic experience includes real estate articles for local, state and national magazines. As a contributing writer, her real estate information has been published in the *Chattanooga Times Free Press*. As Research Editor she collected and edited information for *Twenty Years and More*, the history of Central Baptist Church, Chattanooga, Tennessee.

Appreciation goes to Bill McLaughlin, my life-long friend from Halls, Tennessee, whom I hold in high esteem, for his suggestions and encouragement to complete this book.

Thanks go to Sandi Case, our faithful friend and capable secretary, who has entered the text of the stories on the computer – over and over again – as we revised and edited the content of the book.

We are thankful for the love and care of our Heavenly Father who has sustained and guided us through the years as we lived our Christian faith and raised our children to love and honor Him.

FOREWORD

Telling stories about my early childhood, the humorous adventures of my youth and my family and business experiences gives me great pleasure.

Retelling the stories and confirming the information for *It's A Long Way From Halls* brought the events of the past that shaped my life vividly to my memory.

During the depression years my parents struggled to provide for the family. In spite of our meager existence, my brother Bob and I were healthy, happy children. As a teenager, I was full of energy and optimism for the years that lay ahead. In my adult years working diligently to provide for my family and to achieve success in my personal and business relationships has given me personal satisfaction.

The collection of stories in *It's A Long Way From Halls* is written as a heritage for my children and grandchildren. Hopefully, this book will inspire its readers to record their own stories and experiences as a legacy for their families and future generations.

CONTENTS

Chapter 1 – THE EARLY YEARS
Poised for life   23
Living with Grandparents   25

Chapter 2 – ELEMENTARY SCHOOL YEARS
My First Job   27
A Lawnmower Purchase   28
Bicycle for Sale   29
Childhood Chums   30

Chapter 3 – THE DEPRESSION YEARS
Dad Gets a Job   31
Duplex Purchase   32
Family Separation   33

Chapter 4 – VARIETY IS THE SPICE OF LIFE
Going Hog Wild   35
Extra! Extra! Read All About It!   37
Cotton Patches and Soda Pop   38
My Restaurant Training   40

Chapter 5 – HIGH SCHOOL HIGHLIGHTS
Army Air Force Base in Halls   41
My Activities in Sports   43
Youth Pastor at Halls First Baptist Church   48

Chapter 6 – OFF TO COLLEGE
Union University   51
A Variety of Jobs   51

Chapter 7 – HALE'S GROCERY

Buying the Grocery Store 53
Bill McLaughlin Employed 57
Delivery Boy on a Bicycle 58
My First Car 58
Buying a Home in Halls 60

Chapter 8 – NIFTY FIFTIES

A Memphis State College Education 63
Joining Kappa Sigma Fraternity 64
Accepted in the Air Force ROTC Program 66
Along Came Ann 67
Dancing to the "Big Bands" of the Fifties 69
Our Engagement and Wedding 70
"Three Little Fishes" – On Our Honeymoon 72
Watermelons for Sale 73
Selling Electrolux Vacuum Cleaners 76
My Favorite Electrolux Sales 81
Our Money – in the Stock Market?!? 84
"Off We Go" – into the Air Force 85

Chapter 9 – CHOOSING A CAREER

A New Career in Real Estate 89
Trading Homes in Real Estate 92
Carrie Comes to Clean and Care 94
Hale Realty is Established 95
Dale Carnegie Course Graduate 104
Bill McLaughlin Joins Hale Realty 104
Ledford's Service Station is Sold 108

Chapter 10 – EXPANDING IN BUSINESS
A New Home for Hale Realty   111
Tom and Tim – My Faithful Helpers   114
President Chattanooga Association of Realtors   116
Hamilton County Baptist Association   118
President Woodmore Elementary School PTA   120
President Tennessee Association of Realtors   123
Surviving a Hurricane in Mexico   129

Chapter 11 – FAMILY ADVENTURES
And the Floods Came!   133
Vacations at Daytona Beach, Florida   135
Our Daughters are off to College   138

Chapter 12 – SUCCESSFUL SEVENTIES
Developing the Ledford Farmland   141
Celebrating Anniversaries   146
Central Baptist Church Celebrates
    "Twenty Years and More"   147
"Mr. Roy" Honors REALTORS   149
Chattanooga Board of REALTORS Builds Office   151

Chapter 13 – Our Daughters Say "I Do"   153

Chapter 14 – POTPOURRI
National WCR Installation   161
Halls Homecoming 1986   162
Pat Rose Elected Commissioner   166
Chattanooga Association of REALTORS
    Celebrates Its "Diamond Jubilee"   167
Returning to Hawaii   169

Chapter 15 – MOVING TO EAST BRAINERD
A New Location for Hale Realty 171
Ann Receives Honors 176
Real Estate Company Merger 179
Pilgrimage to the Holy Land 181
Ledford Apartments Damaged by Tornado 184

Chapter 16 – ENTERING THE TWENTY-FIRST CENTURY
Millennial Year of 2000 189
Designation as *REALTOR Emeritus* 193
Traveling Buddies Through the Years 193
Our Golden Wedding Anniversary 194

Chapter 17 – LET ME TELL YOU ABOUT MY GRANDCHILDREN
Jennifer Susan Chastain 199
Brad Franklin Chastain 203
Brandon Douglas Bunn 205
Tyler Durand Bunn 207
Davis Alexander Bunn 211
Cameron Michael Gonzalez 213
Alex Christopher Gonzalez 217

Chapter 18 –EIGHTIETH BIRTHDAY 219

Chapter 19 – LIFE IS GOOD 223

A Salesman's Prayer 224
Attitude for Success 225
A word from Bill McLaughlin 226

Illustrations

Halls signs	*Frontispiece*
Dub age 2	22
Dub age 6 and Bob age 3	24
Peery grandparents	25
Dub age 8	27
First bicycle	29
Dad and boys on crane	31
First duplex	32
Dad, Mom, Bob and Dub	34
Lonnie & Charlie Viar	35
Bob 11 and Dub 14	38
B-17 at Halls	41
Wymond Hurt, Jr.	42
Charlie Viar	44
Dub football player	45
Dub high school senior	46
Halls High School class of 1946	47
First Baptist Church at Halls	49
Youth pastor	50
Hale's Grocery interior	52
Hale's Grocery front	55
Hometown USA	56
Hale's Grocery entrance	56
Bill McLaughlin age 10	57
Duplex on College Street	59

The Hales at second grocery   60

Pauline and Raymond Hale   61

Dub as college freshman   63

Kappa Sigma fraternity   64

Vice- president of class   64

John McNail   65

Joining Air Force ROTC   66

First date   67

Pinmates   68

Mary Ann Ledford betrothed   70

Bride, groom and parents   71

Home on Barbara Circle   73

Electrolux business card   77

"Electrolux News"   79

Waldorf-Astoria 1953   80

Kenny Sinks   80

Electrolux Awards 1954   81

Dub and Ann as graduates   85

Commissioned Lieutenant   86

Family portrait 1956   87

Fike Realty business card   90

Woodmore Terrace home   93

Carrie Davenport   95

Hale Realty first office   96

Collins Circle home   97

Waverly Park announcement 99

Morris Estates 100

Lakebrook 101

Six Hale girls 102

Plemons Estates 103

Dale Carnegie diploma 105

Bill and Martha McLaughlin 106

Mr. and Mrs. Ledford 108

Carl Martin KFC 109

New office building 110

The Hale Building 111

Ribbon cutting 1967 112

Agents and staff on dedication day 113

Family celebration 114

Tim Johnson 115

President Chattanooga Association of REALTORS 117

Hamilton County Baptist Association 119

Governor Winfield Dunn 124

Linda Woods and Steve Harding 125

Forrest Cate, Jr. and Romulus 126

Tennessee luau 128

Tennessee Realtor magazine 128

REALTOR of the Year 1974 131

Flood on Shawhan Road 133

Albert and Alice Waller 134

Marineland, Florida, 1966 135

Disney World 1972   136

"Miss Beauty-less"   137

7024 Pauline Circle   139

7022 Pauline Circle   139

Ledford Apartments   140

Ledford Apartments construction   141

Blueprints Ledford Apartments   142

Roy Kincer   144

Lamar Williams   144

Ledford tenant picnic   145

Ledford golden anniversary   146

Hale silver anniversary   147

Central Baptist Church   148

Mr. & Mrs. Roy McDonald   148

Chattanooga News-Free Press tour   150

New Board of REALTORS building   151

Joan and David wedding portrait   154

Susan and Mitchell wedding portrait   155

Dianne and Michael wedding portrait   156

Viar family   157

Ann's school friends   158

Friends at wedding   159

Waller family   160

Bettye and George Harrison   161

Packing for Halls reunion   162

Jim and Mary Ann Peery   163

Hurt family at Halls First Baptist 164

Halls High School 40th reunion 165

Pat Rose campaign 166

Eddie Nicholson at Diamond Jubilee 168

Kellye Cash, Miss Tennessee 168

Dinner in Hawaii 169

"Dancing with the Stars" 170

Hale Realty on East Brainerd Road 171

Vernon Cox 172

Dianne and Cameron 173

Sandi Case and family 174

"Kids On The Block" 175

Pat Boone 175

Wall of Presidents 176

Ann Member of the Year 1989 177

Ann REALTOR of the Year 1991 179

Hale Realty Awards banquet 180

Hale/Elgin Smith merger 181

Sea of Galilee 182

Masada 183

Tornado damage 185

$20.00 bills 187

Ledford Apartments Pool 188

Ann installed as president 190

Daughters and sons-in-law 190

Washington Legislative Conference 191

REALTOR Emeritus	192
Poss and Bettye Powell	194
Golden wedding anniversary	195
Church friends at the celebration	196
Family portrait June 22, 2002	197
School friends at the celebration	198
"Miss Bess T. Shepherd" Award	200
Jennifer Susan Chastain	201
Brad Franklin Chastain	202
Brad in first grade	204
Brandon Douglas Bunn	205
Brandon's golf swing	206
Tyler Durand Bunn	207
After the hole-in-one	210
Three grandsons	210
Davis Alexander Bunn	211
Twins Tyler and Davis	212
Cameron Michael Gonzalez	215
Alex Christopher Gonzalez	216
Alex and Cameron with guitars	218
Raymond and Ann, 80th birthday party	219
Bunn Family	220
Chastain Family	220
Gonzalez Family	221
Mr. and Mrs. Beck	221
Raymond Franklin Hale, Jr. at age 80	222

Raymond Franklin Hale, Jr., "Dub", at two years old.

Chapter 1
THE EARLY YEARS

Poised for Life

At two years of age, I posed for my first photograph. A professional photographer traveled through the small towns and rural communities of West Tennessee taking pictures of children and families. My mother had me ready for his arrival. I was "scrubbed", with a fresh haircut, polished shoes, and a new suit. While I was in good shape, the porch on which I sat was not. The boards in the porch were rotting away and the concrete steps were cracked on this rental house we called home.

Times were hard during the depression years when I was born. The place of my birth was Halls, Tennessee, a small farming community in northwest Tennessee. I was born on January 27, 1929, to Pauline Peery Hale and Raymond Franklin Hale, Sr. and named Raymond Franklin Hale, Jr. My birth was at home as was customary in the rural communities where medical facilities were not available. Weighing barely five pounds and struggling to live, my survival was questionable. My Dad tagged me with the nickname of "Dub." The

Raymond Franklin Hale, Jr. (age 6) and Robert Lee Hale (age 3)

birth of my brother, Robert Lee Hale, on April 8, 1932, made our family complete.

As my parents established a home with two little boys, times continued to be difficult as they were for many families.

Living with Grandparents

When Bob and I were young our family moved almost every year. Dad could not keep the rent paid because finding and holding a job was hard for him. We often lived with our grandparents, Alice and John Cody Peery. My favorite memory of Granddaddy is sharing time with him popping corn over an open fireplace. My grandparents' mode of transportation

Alice and John Peery, "Dub's" Grandparents, with prized possessions – a mule and wagon.

was a mule and wagon and riding with them on trips into town was a special treat. I looked forward to each week. Grandparents provide the warmth of love, a sense of stability and many happy memories – as they did for Bob and me.

Chapter 2
ELEMENTARY SCHOOL YEARS

My First Job

When I was in elementary school a variety of small jobs were available and my goal was to work hard and please the people who hired me. My first job at eight years of age was helping the lady next door, a senior citizen, by bringing in coal, kindling and wood for the fireplace. Her brother, who lived across town, hired me for a nickel a day to help keep her home warm. I was thrilled with the pay because in the "good ole" days one could go to the movie for a dime and buy a Coke and popcorn for a nickel each. On Saturday

At eight years of age, "Dub" has his first job.

friends would join me and we could enjoy an after-noon at the movie.

A Lawnmower Purchase

At ten years of age, after borrowing $6.35 from my Dad and buying a push lawnmower, several neighbors agreed for me to mow their yards. The largest yard in town was cut for a quarter. By the end of the summer, the money borrowed for the lawnmower was repaid to my dad and extra dollars were saved in my "piggy" bank.

One of my most vivid memories of mowing yards was while cutting grass for Mrs. Leonard Andrews whose husband owned the drugstore on Main Street. Her lot was large and she was being charged a quarter.

The lady next door came over and asked, "What will you charge for cutting my yard? It's not as big as the one you are doing now." We agreed on fifteen cents and she went into her house. When she returned to the porch the front yard was finished and the back-yard was being cut.

I told her, "I'll be through here in a few minutes."

When the mowing was complete the yard passed her critical inspection. She exclaimed, "Well, I'm not going to pay you fifteen cents because that's too much for a little boy to make in a few minutes."

I asked, "What are you going to pay me?"

"I'll pay you a dime," she answered.

After responding with a dejected "okay" and accepting the dime, cutting her grass was never again on my mowing schedule.

Bicycle for Sale

When I was ten years old, I received my first bicycle at Christmastime. The cost of the bicycle was $20.95. After riding the bike over the streets of Halls for four years, it was sold for $20. With such a good sale, the cost of using it was only 95 cents. The bicycle deal was an indicator of the way my life in sales would develop at a later time.

A gift of a bicycle pleased "Dub" at ten years of age.

Childhood Chums

In my elementary school years, occasional weekends were spent on the farm with friends Bobby and Billy Steelman. For entertainment we rode horses, mules and calves and played football in the fields. "Country-cooking" dinners prepared from the Steelman's vegetable gardens were special treats. One does not forget the wonderful times shared with friends when life was simpler.

Chapter 3
THE DEPRESSION YEARS

Dad Gets a Job

In the depression years life was difficult and jobs were few. Dad found odd jobs in Nankipoo, a small community several miles from Halls. He walked to work and home each day. The walk and hours were long and the pay was meager.

As children, "Dub" and Bob enjoyed rides on a construction crane at their dad's worksite.

In the 1930's after Franklin D. Roosevelt was elected U.S. President, the government provided jobs on public works projects and Dad was hired as a crane operator in Memphis, Tennessee. Occasionally, Bob and I would go with him to work and ride the crane. This was a special treat for us.

Duplex purchased in 1937 by Raymond Hale, Sr.

Duplex Purchase

By 1937, when I was in third grade, Dad had accumulated enough money to make a down payment on a duplex that was damaged by fire. He worked on the duplex six or eight months before we moved into the right side. Dad rented the left side for $11.50 per month. The mortgage payment was $11.75.

After several years, my family was having a tough time financially and foreclosure on the duplex seemed likely. I remember hearing Mother and Daddy talking about paying the mortgage that was three months delinquent.

They were asking "What are we going to do? What can we do? We need to make the payments."

The bank officer agreed if Dad paid one month's payment of $11.75 and kept the future payments current, the bank would give him time to make the back payments. I went to my "piggy" bank and took out enough money to make the one payment required by the bank. This was my first experience in helping to pay the mortgage.

Family Separation

When Dad worked in Memphis as a heavy equipment operator with public works, he and Mother became estranged and separated. He was not at home through my junior and senior high school years, nor did he provide financial support for our family.

Mother worked at a dry goods store and a tomato canning factory to help support the family. The factory was crowded and steamy with hot vats of tomatoes. Women wore "sweat bands" on their foreheads and scooped tomatoes from the huge containers with their hands. The tomatoes were "skinned" and passed to the next group of workers to continue the processing and canning.

One hot summer afternoon my brother and I went by the factory to see our Mom and saw the terrible working conditions. I vowed to get her out of there by providing another source of income for our family.

Dad Raymond, Mother Polly, Bob and "Dub" in happier days.

Chapter 4
VARIETY IS THE SPICE OF LIFE

Going Hog Wild

The Depression continued through the 1930's and in 1937 when I was eight years old, times were hard for my family. My Uncle Lonnie Viar, Sr., was a land own-

Uncle Lonnie Viar, Sr. and Cousin Charlie Viar are among rows of corn on their Knob Creek farm near Halls.

er and farmer who raised hogs for sale and slaughter. His son Charlie, who is four years older than I, came by my home for a visit.

Charlie asked me, "Dub, would you like to have a few pigs?

The weather is bad and the large animals are trampling them. They're only selling for two cents a pound but I would be glad to give you a couple of pigs."

"Well, Charlie, where are we going to put them?" I asked. "I can't put them in the house and we don't have a hog pen."

"I'll take care of that," he said.

Charlie came by with several farm helpers, built a hog pen, and gave me two pigs – a sow and a boar. To feed them, I gathered slop (discarded food and liquids) from a nearby boarding house.

The sow had eleven pigs and seven of them lived. The winter was extremely cold and the pigs would have died if left outside. They were cared for by wrapping them in cloths and bottle feeding them for two weeks. They were kept on the back porch until strong enough to go back to the hog pen.

The hogs were raised until they were what we called "topping out" at the weight they would be most tender

– about 240 pounds. Mother, Dad, Bob and I slaughtered one hog during the first cold spell in November. We blocked out the hams, carved out the shoulders and salted the meat for curing in the smokehouse. The pork chops, ground sausage and streak-o-lean were refrigerated. For the remainder of the year we had meat for our family.

We sold eight hogs for a profit. Raising hogs was my first business venture.

Extra! Extra! Read All About It!

In the seventh grade, I took a job delivering 150 newspapers every morning. The papers – *The Commercial Appeal* – were brought from Memphis and dropped off at three locations in town.

My mother waked me at 5 A.M. and I'd pick up my papers, fold them, put them in a bag, then deliver them by 7 A.M. The papers were delivered on my bicycle. Sometimes walking was easier because there were steep hills and it was hard to carry the papers on my bicycle. After completing my paper route, I would go home, have breakfast and walk across the street to school.

Uncle Lonnie Viar, who was on my paper route, called the first afternoon when he returned home from his farm. He lived in the city and would drive to his farm four or five miles away every day.

He asked, "Dub, can you get my paper here a little bit earlier?"

I said, "Well, I sure can, Uncle Lonnie."

"You know, I go to work on the farm at 6:00 A.M. I sure would like to have my paper before leaving," he explained.

"Okay, I'll take care of that," was my response. The thought occurred to me of reversing my paper route and getting Uncle Lonnie's paper to him at a quarter of 6:00 in the morning. The change of schedule worked just great and he was pleased to have his newspaper before daylight.

Cotton Patches and Soda Pop

In the fall of the year school closed for a month while the crops were gathered and cotton was picked. My brother Bob and I walked to town and waited on the street corner

Bob at 11 and "Dub" at 14 years of age.

to catch a truck going to the cotton fields about 7 A.M. In the 1930's a worker could make 50 cents for picking one hundred pounds of cotton. After picking two hundred pounds a day, I earned a dollar. At the end of a long, hot day, Bob and I rode the cotton wagon back to town.

After a day in the cotton patches, I'd go home, clean up and go to the drug store to "jerk" sodas from 6 P.M. until midnight. I mixed milk shakes, made sundaes, served Cokes and limeades. On my first day the owner left me in charge while he went home for lunch. Kathleen, a classmate, came in the drugstore and ordered a limeade. No one else was in the drugstore.

Leaning over the counter I whispered, "Kathleen, how do you make a limeade?"

She said, "Give me fizzy water with a little lime in it." (Kathleen forgot to tell me to add sweetening syrup). I took the drink to her table then peeked over the counter to see if she liked it. She was making a horrible face.

"Kathleen, what's wrong?" I asked.

"You didn't put any sugar in this limeade," she answered.

Sweetener was added to the limeade and the customer made very happy. My first lesson in preparing soda fountain drinks – don't forget the sweetener. For a day's work at the drugstore my pay was a dollar and all I could eat and drink.

My Restaurant Training

In the summer after eighth grade, I worked in a restaurant owned by Ed Stansfield. What was good news for me was bad news for the young man who left the restaurant for two weeks training at a National Guard camp. While he was away I substituted for him as a waiter. When he returned he told Mr. Ed, "I'll be back to work on Monday morning."

"Well, I don't believe you need to come back. I'm going to hire Dub to take your place for the next two months," Mr. Ed informed him.

Mr. Ed taught me to meet people, wait on them and thank them for eating at his place – good public relations training for my future job at "The Normal Tea Room", a restaurant in Memphis near the Memphis State College campus.

Chapter 5
HIGH SCHOOL HIGHLIGHTS

Army Air Force Base in Halls

As the dark clouds of war gathered over the world, the Japanese bombed Pearl Harbor on December 7, 1941, and brought America into World War II.

Our small town of Halls was changed from a slow-paced farm community to a strategic location for an

A B-17 Air Force training base was located in Halls from 1942-1945.

Army Air Base. The Air Base was built in 1942 to train B-17 bomber pilots and crew members scheduled to fly bombing missions overseas. This brought more than a thousand people into the town and significantly improved the economy.

During the war years, families rented rooms to airmen and their wives so they could be together the last five or six weeks before the men were sent into combat. The Air Base was the last stop stateside for the airmen.

Wymond Hurt, Jr., with his Chevrolet Coupe.

The drug store where I worked in high school was a gathering place for the airmen. My friends and I had a good time getting to know the servicemen. After they left Halls for overseas, we would often hear the tragic news they were killed in action. It was a sad time for all.

Mr. and Mrs. Wymond Hurt, Sr., rented a room to an officer stationed at the Air Base. When the officer left to go overseas in December 1944, he left his convertible with the Hurts and gave permission for their son to drive it once a week.

Their son, Wymond, was one of my best high school friends, so I would go with him on his weekly ride. We'd go dating in the convertible and visit the girls in the surrounding towns.

My Activities in Sports

I enrolled in Halls High School in September 1942 and graduated in June 1946. Being a good football player, I managed to make the first string three years in a row, which were my sophomore, junior and senior years. The team selected me as cocaptain my senior year and my position was quarterback.

We played schools much larger than Halls, which had a population of 2,000. Jackson had 30,000 people and Dyersburg had 15,000. Competing with the big schools was difficult. We traveled to the neighboring towns in a one-and-a-half ton truck with a tarpau-

Following his high school years Charlie Viar joined the Marines.

lin over the top. During those years we could not use the school buses because of the gas shortage. During the war years the high school did not have funds to buy football uniforms and equipment, so the players wore jerseys, pants and shoes left over from other teams. Everybody had to really conserve during the second World War.

One night in my freshman year we played Brownsville. My cousin, Charlie Viar, mentioned earlier, was a senior and one of the largest boys on our team. Charlie was hurt during the last quarter of the game and was lying on the ground on the sidelines. I went over to see if I could make him feel better. He had broken his leg in two places, but we didn't know that until after the game was over and he was taken to the doctor.

"Dub" Hale played football at Halls High School in the mid 1940's.

During the last quarter three or four other guys were also hurt. My friend, Wymond Hurt, and I were sitting on the bench. We looked over at those big old boys crying because they were all beat up. The coach didn't have anybody else to play, so he came over to me and Wymond.

"Hale, do you want to go in?" he asked.

I said, "No, sir, Mr. Ammons, I don't believe I want to go in."

He looked at Hurt, and asked, "You want to go in, Hurt?"

"No. I don't believe I want to go in, either," he answered. So, needless to

A senior in high school, "Dub" was honored for his leadership ability.

say, we didn't go in the game to play that night. The Brownsville team beat us 38 to 0!

On Monday when we went out for practice the coach said, "Well, I'll tell you boys who didn't want to play the other night that I'm going to let you run this football track at Halls High for the next two hours." So we ran track and ran track until we almost fell out. The next time the coach asked us to go in and play, we said "Yes, Sir!"

In a game in my junior year I punted the football eighty three yards. This is a record that still stands at Halls High School. No one has kicked a football any farther since this record was established in 1944.

In my senior year we played the high school in Jackson, Tennessee, which had four teams dressed out.

Halls only had fifteen men dressed to play even though there were twenty on the team. Halls knew Jackson was tough, so we went to the game with only fifteen players because five of them were afraid to play. One player had his front teeth knocked out and the guy that hit him looked at another player and shouted, "You're going to be next."

We ran scared and lost 52-0. After the game we hurried to the truck and headed for Halls. Coach Ammons stopped at a restaurant and gave us twenty-five cents each to buy a couple of hamburgers and a Coke. He was a kind coach and wonderful mentor.

Halls High School Class of 1946

Mr. Ammons also coached the basketball team. For three years I was on the first string basketball team and was honored as Captain my senior year.

Twenty-eight students graduated from Halls High School in the Class of '46. At graduation time I was honored by being voted "Best Athlete," "Most Friendly" and "Most Likely to Succeed."

As my high school years ended, so did the second World War. Japan surrendered to the Allied Powers in August of 1945. We were optimistic that peace and prosperity were in our future.

Youth Pastor at Halls First Baptist Church

My family joined Halls First Baptist Church when I was ten years old and during a weekly revival I accepted Christ as my Savior. One of the most influential people in my life was my Sunday School teacher, Mrs. Rebecca Burnett, who encouraged me in my Christian life.

In the spring of 1946, Halls First Baptist Church scheduled a Youth Revival. When the revival was announced, the Pastor asked me to be Youth Pastor for the week. Mother encouraged me to accept the responsibility and said, "You may be an influence on other young people."

After agreeing to serve as Youth Pastor for the week, I prepared a sermon, led a deacons' meeting, attended a Finance Committee meeting and visited church prospects. These are also ways of serving churches in my adult life. Following the Sunday morning service, two young men visiting the church stepped forward at the invitation to confess their sins, accept Christ as Savior and join the church.

My Aunt Mabel Peery attended the service. Afterward she complimented my message, hugged me and slipped $5 in my hand. Five dollars was more than I made working all day! Her generosity was appreciated and the gift assisted me in school.

First Baptist Church of Halls

"Dub" served as Youth Pastor at Halls First Baptist Church in April 1946.

Chapter 6
OFF TO COLLEGE

Union University

Deciding to continue my education, I enrolled at Union University, a Baptist College in Jackson. Tennessee, in September of 1946. Mother and Dad had been separated for several years and there was no money, help or support for college. To go to Jackson, enroll in Union University, get a job and put myself through school was my commitment and goal.

A Variety of Jobs

While at Union and living in the boys' dormitory I picked up laundry and cleaning for extra dollars. From 1-6 P.M. at Five-Point Lumber Company I worked with big, muscular guys twice my size unloading lumber from boxcars. This job brought in extra dollars but it was too hard for me.

Searching for other employment I went to the local A & P Supermarket several times asking for work before the manager gave me a job in the meat department. He taught me how to prepare the meat, stock the meat counter, and wait on customers. Working at the supermarket for four months was a beneficial experience when I later owned my own grocery store.

Hale's Grocery: Bob Hale, Jimmy Mosely, "Dub" Hale and Raymond Hale, Sr. are pictured with customers in 1948.

Chapter 7
HALE'S GROCERY

Buying the Grocery Store

When the second quarter of college was over on March 10, 1947, I "hitchhiked" home to Halls and visited the grocery store where I worked part-time for a couple of years in high school. The elderly owner, Bud Studdard, and his son-in-law, Jack Davis, mentioned they wanted to sell the grocery and retire.

As we talked I asked, "Well, what do you want for it?"

They said, "Only $2900 for the stock and fixtures."

"I don't have any money – only $150 to go back to college next quarter," I responded.

"Maybe you can borrow it," they suggested.

At eighteen years of age, I went to the Bank of Halls, told the President my story and asked to borrow $2900 to buy the grocery store. To "sell" him on the idea that I would be successful and pay back the money was my goal.

He listened carefully, looked up and said, "Son, I can't let you have any money until you are twenty-one years of age."

Being turned down for a loan was a big disappointment. Not to be defeated, a call was made to my Uncle Lonnie Viar. Remember, in the seventh grade I delivered his morning paper before 6 A.M. when he left to go to his farm. He was pleased his wish to get his paper early was granted.

When I called him, he said, "Come by tomorrow evening about 5 P.M."

While talking with him I told him, "I need to borrow $2900 to buy the stock and fixtures of the grocery store owned by Mr. Stoddard and Mr. Davis."

"I believe I can help you with the purchase," he stated. "Go ahead and make your deal and when you get ready for the money, just call me."

"I'll make my deal in the morning," I told him.

The next evening at his home he gave me $2900. We agreed monthly payments would be made over a period of two years, beginning in the fall. He knew time was needed to build my business and to save money for cash flow. On Friday the thirteenth of March 1947, my mother and I opened HALE'S GROCERY in Halls, Tennessee. My little brother, Bob, helped in the store after school. After a successful ten months in business, I called Uncle Lonnie, met with him and paid in full the balance of the $2900 loan which was $1450.

Hale's Grocery in the background for "Dub" and brother, Bob, as they display "Hog's Delight" for sale.

The grocery building rented for $25 a month was approximately 30' x 30' – about 900 square feet. There was no air conditioning in the hot summer months. The building was heated in the winter by a kerosene heater vented through the ceiling. There was no refrigerated meat box to display meat products, just a refrigerator for sandwich meat. A cigar box was used to hold the cash and make change.

In Memphis, sixty miles away, the big Montessi Supermarket was selling used equipment and purchasing a twelve-foot meat display box put me in the "meat business." The Armour Company delivered meat to the store on Friday morning. A friend who was a butcher with Kroger Company came by on Friday night for several weeks to show me how to cut the meat.

HOMETOWN USA: Halls, Tennessee – The Business District on Front Street bustled with activity on Saturdays in the 40's and 50's with farmers buying and bartering merchandise. The stores included a pool room, small ice cream shop, feed and seed store, Hales's Grocery (double-door building in center) and dry cleaners.

A closer view of the first Hale's Grocery Store entrance is shown at right.

On Friday nights I worked until ten or eleven o'clock to get the meat ready for Saturday sales. Good meat products in a grocery attract customers, and then they buy other items and groceries as well.

In our small farming community, we always did more business on Saturday than all the rest of the week. The store was open and we worked longer hours than other merchants. In a short time, Hale's Grocery doubled its volume of business.

Bill McLaughlin Employed

From the small community of Bruceville, Tennessee, near Halls, the McLaughlin family came to trade at Hale's Grocery. Bill McLaughlin was the youngest of ten children

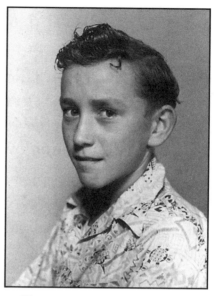

Billy McLaughlin helped at Hale's Grocery at ten years of age.

of sharecroppers. A bright, personable ten year old, he was always ready to help others. The customers gave him their grocery lists to collect items from the shelves to complete their orders.

After several weeks I knew he was a hard worker and could help us. Bill was delighted when offered a job in the store on Saturdays. He was so small his work apron was rolled up several times to keep him from tripping over it.

Bill rode his bike or "hitchhiked" to work but after the store closed at 10 P.M., I took him home to Bruceville. This was the beginning of a life-long friendship I cherish today.

Delivery Boy on a Bicycle

The first six months at Hale's Grocery the groceries were delivered on a bicycle. When customers called and ordered groceries to be delivered to their homes, as was customary in the 1940's, I was the "delivery boy on a bicycle" – I didn't own a car.

An elderly customer lived on a hill a mile and a half from the store. She frequently called to order a case of RC Colas – in sixteen ounce glass bottles – and a five gallon can of oil.

The RC's were placed in the basket on the front of the bike and the oil rode on the back of the bike. If I had an accident, maybe I could hold on to the colas because they were more valuable – the oil could spill on the ground.

Trying to pedal my bike up the hill was difficult. I'd go halfway and stop to rest, and then push the bike to her home at the top of the hill.

I needed a car!

My First Car

After six months in business buying a used car was affordable. One day Mr. Joe Sumrow, a prominent land and cotton gin owner came in town. His wife drove a shiny, black 1939 Chevrolet and I commented, "Now, Mr. Joe, if you ever decide to sell your wife's car, I would like to buy it."

The Hale home on College Street in Halls

After several months passed, Mr. Joe came by the store "bright and early"– 6:30 A.M. – as I was sweeping the front sidewalk and opening the store. He said, "Dub, I am on my way to Memphis to buy my wife a new car. I have her Chevrolet at Mr. White's Service Station to be serviced and cleaned. It's priced at $600. If you want to drive it, you may go by the station and get it."

"Mr. Joe," I said, "I don't want to drive it. I want to buy it!" When Mr. Joe arrived home from Memphis, arrangements had been made for the $600 to pay for the car.

Delivering groceries just got easier!

Dating became easier, too. It's hard to date a girl when you are walking. My girlfriend lived with her brother, an airman, near the Army Air Base and the two mile walk to visit her was long. After purchasing the Chevrolet, my horizons were expanded to the next little town ten miles away to date new girls and make new friends.

Buying a Home in Halls

After establishing a successful business at Hale's Grocery, the time had come to invest in real estate. Mother and I bought the house next to our duplex for $4,000 and moved into it in late summer of 1948. The duplex became investment property.

Dub's parents in front of the second Hale's Grocery

In the fall of 1949 Dad returned home after more than ten years away. His car was repossessed, he was penniless – he had nothing. There was no money for rent, so he was looking for a place to call home.

Mother and I allowed him to come home with a few "ground rules" – no alcohol and he was to help us in the store.

Dad was happy to be home with Mother, Bob and me. He worked at Hale's Grocery, attended church with us and turned his life around to become a faithful husband and loving dad.

Dub's parents, Pauline Peery Hale and Raymond Franklin Hale, Sr., in a 1950 portrait

Chapter 8
NIFTY FIFTIES

A Memphis State College Education

After being in the grocery business three and a half years, time had come to return to college. Mother was a great encourager for me to receive more education.

In the fall of 1950, I enrolled in Memphis State College where my brother Bob attended. Hale's Grocery provided financial support for us to live and complete our educations. On Friday afternoon after classes, we went home to Halls and worked in the store with our parents until ten or eleven o'clock at night. Saturdays were always long days as well.

On Sundays Bob and I attended Halls

"Dub" Hale enrolled in Memphis State College in the fall of 1950. He joined Kappa Sigma Fraternity and was elected Pledge Class President.

First Baptist Church with our parents, and enjoyed a "home-cooked" dinner of fried chicken, hot biscuits and chocolate pie. Then it was time to head back to Memphis for another week of classes.

Joining Kappa Sigma Fraternity

Kappa Sigma Fraternity pledge class

Junior class officers at Memphis State were, left to right: Marilyn Sanford, Ronnie Gruenwald, "Dub" Hale, and Bobby Reed.

On arriving at Memphis State College, I was invited to join the Kappa Sigma Fraternity. Being elected president of the Pledge Class gave me opportunities to make new friends and develop leadership skills. I held several offices in the fraternity and was also elected vice-president of the class in my junior year.

One of my best college friends and fraternity buddies was John McNail from Milan, Tennessee. He lived in the boarding house near the campus where we shared "room and board" with ten other students. John and I had several classes together, double-dated and enjoyed many good times together.

In August of 1952, after Ann and I were married in June, John came to visit us in Halls. Joan Speakman, Ann's friend, was also visiting and we had a memo-

Fraternity brothers, John McNail and "Dub" Hale

rable evening showing our friends the town of Halls, having dinner and dancing at the VFW Club.

John was returning to Milan late that evening when he went to sleep and drove off a bridge. In this tragic accident he lost his leg and spent many months in the hospital and rehabilitation. He did not return to college, but joined his dad in the banking business and became president of Farmer's Peoples Bank in Milan, Tennessee.

Accepted in the Air Force ROTC Program

An Air Force Reserve Officers Training Corps (ROTC) unit was formed at Memphis State College

First row: Col. Oscar Thomas and Lt. Col. Joe Allen. In second row, left to right: Majors Robert Pruitt, Don Rhoads, William Satterfield, Dub Hale and James Holcomb. In back row, Sgt. James Myers and Sgt. William Simpson.

my freshman year. The Korean War (1950-1953) was raging and men were expecting to be drafted into the Army, so they were volunteering for their favorite branch of service or choosing ROTC training in college. The ROTC program at Memphis State College was my choice with the goal of entering the Air Force after graduation.

Along Came Ann

While in Memphis during the week, I worked at a restaurant – The Normal Tea Room – through the busy hours of 11 A.M. until 2 P.M. and 5 P.M. until 8 P.M.

"Dub" and Ann's first date on December 6, 1951, was for dinner at a friend's house – served "Pheasant Under Glass" – and dancing with friends, Jackie Haslett and John McNail at the Flamingo Club.

One night a little brunette came in for dinner and I rushed to wait on her. She stopped in the restaurant often and we became acquainted. She also attended Memphis State College and lived across the street from the campus.

Ann's first trip to Halls, Tennessee, to meet "Dub's" parents was February 10, 1952. Raymond and Ann are pictured at the Hale's home on College Street.

Her name was ANN.

Ann accepted my invitation when asked for a date. Our first date was a dinner at the home of a friend. In elegant style we were served "pheasant under glass" by candlelight. Following a lovely dinner, we danced with friends to a lively band at the Flamingo Club. The "big band" sound became our favorite music.

Ann and I dated until the Christmas holidays. During Christmas vacation she returned to Chattanooga – and a boyfriend – and I went to Halls for the holidays to work in the store. My expectation was that Ann would get an engagement ring for Christmas. The day after Christmas I called and asked, "Well, did you get that ring for Christmas?"

When she answered "No", I was "home free" since the other guy was in Chattanooga and I was in Memphis near her. This arrangement was a "winner" and worked well for me.

We dated through January and February when she accepted my Kappa Sigma fraternity pin to wear with her Chi Omega pin. "Pinning" was a college tradition of the 1950's. When you were "going steady" your girlfriend accepted your fraternity pin and wore it with her sorority pin.

Dancing to the "Big Bands" of the Fifties

The ultimate destination for dating and dancing was the Skyway Room where the "big bands" of the fifties, including Tommy and Jimmy Dorsey, Shep Fields and Artie Shaw, played high atop the famed Peabody Hotel overlooking the Mississippi River. Ann and I often went dancing to the big bands and enjoyed refreshments which included a container of ice for 50 cents and two Cokes at 25 cents each.

My friend was Public Relations Director for the Peabody Hotel. After selling him a vacuum cleaner, I gave him bags and accessories for his machine in exchange for "passes" to the Peabody's Skyway Room. The best deal in this arrangement was mine – dancing is much more fun than vacuuming!

Our Engagement and Wedding

In March Ann and I went to Chattanooga for me to meet her parents, Edith and Durand Ledford. After asking her Dad's permission for us to marry, her parents tried to discourage us from marrying until we finished college. The Ledfords were not very good salespeople because we didn't change our minds but promised to finish school. They gave their permission for a summer wedding and in April we became engaged.

Mary Ann Ledford of Chattanooga, Tennessee, became engaged in April 1952 to marry Raymond F. "Dub" Hale, Jr. of Halls, Tennessee.

Ann and I married in Chattanooga, Tennessee, on Sunday, June 22, 1952, at Central Baptist Church on McCallie Avenue with Ann's uncle, Dr. Charles L. Norton, Director of the Tennessee Baptist

Raymond "Dub" Hale married Mary Ann Ledford on June 22, 1952, at Central Baptist Church in Chattanooga, Tennessee. Pictured with the bride and groom are C.D. and Edith Ledford, parents of the bride, and Raymond, Sr. and Pauline Hale, parents of the groom.

Convention, and the Reverend Ansell T. Baker offici-
ating. The temperature on our wedding day was over
100 degrees – one of the hottest days of the summer.
There was no air-conditioning in the church and the
candles melted, as is evident in our wedding pictures,
as we said our marriage vows.

"Three Little Fishes" – On Our Honeymoon

Our "honeymoon trip" was to Daytona Beach,
Florida. The mischief of our friends was evident when
we arrived at the beach. After a day in the sun a horrible "fish smell" permeated our car. Ann and I searched
and sniffed to try and find the source of this obnox-
ious odor. Could it be our bathing suits and the beach
towels? Everything was laundered to eliminate the
smell but nothing worked.

The following day we could hardly stand to be in
the car. I drove to a service station and told the atten-
dant there was something wrong with my car. Together we discovered our jolly friends had put fish in the
hubcaps. After three days the "fishes" were well-done
– and very spoiled.

After having the car washed and the hubcaps
cleaned, we went happily on our way – only to get
stuck in the loose sand as we drove on Daytona Beach.
A tow truck pulled us to firmer ground and we headed
for our next adventure. After fifty-six years Daytona
Beach remains our favorite vacation destination.

We met in November, were "pinned" in February, engaged in April and married in June. Truly a whirl-wind romance!

Watermelons for Sale

"Dub" and Ann's first home was a duplex at 3609 Barbara Circle, Memphis, Tennessee, near Memphis State College.

Ann and I returned to Halls from our honeymoon in Daytona Beach, Florida, on the fourth of July 1952. We lived with my parents until September when we returned to Memphis State College and rented a duplex on Barbara Circle near the campus.

Until time to return to college I continued to sell Electrolux vacuum cleaners and work in the grocery store. Fresh summer produce, including watermelons, attracted families to Hale's Grocery. After we were out late with friends one evening, I announced to Ann I was getting up at 1:30 A.M. to go to the Memphis Farmers Market to buy peaches, beans, turnip greens – and watermelons.

"Can I go with you to market?" Ann asked.

"No. You just stay here and I'll be back by noon," I replied.

She insisted on making the trip to Memphis with me. With a two-wheel trailer attached to the pick-up truck, off we went arriving at the market about 3:30 A.M. There were over fifty long-haul trailers loaded with watermelons. A farmer's goal was to sell the melons by the trailer load, if possible. I jumped on the back of an 18-wheeler loaded with 2000+ watermelons and asked, "What will you take for the whole load?"

"I'll take 15 cents a round for the load," the farmer answered.

"Well, I don't think my truck is big enough to haul that many watermelons. What will you charge me by the melon?" I asked.

He responded, "I'll have to have 20 cents each for them."

I bargained, "If you'll let me pick 'em, I'll buy 'em."

It's a done deal!

After backing up my pick-up truck and trailer to the long-haul and choosing the perfect looking watermelons, Ann and I stopped for a quick breakfast and went to the Electrolux office. Six vacuum cleaners fit neatly between us in the cab of the truck. Putting them in the trailer gave me an uneasy feeling because the wind could blow them onto the highway and they would be damaged or lost.

Willie Nelson's "On the Road Again" could have been our theme song as we headed for Halls. After driving about thirty miles, the left wheel came off the two-wheel trailer. The truck coasted to the side of the road as the wheel rolled down a slope and into a ditch. Ann was given instructions to sit on a hillside nearby so if someone hit the truck both of us would not be killed. With her perched on the hill and me by the side of the road, travelers began to stop.

"Can we help you?" they asked.

"Yes. If you don't mind," I said, "How about selling you two watermelons for a dollar?"

After selling thirty to forty melons and emptying the two-wheel trailer, I retrieved the wheel from the ditch and located wire to make the repairs.

I called to Ann, "I'm going to lift the side of the trailer and if you'll come pick up the wheel and bring it to me, I'll wire it back on the axle."

The trailer was heavy but I managed to lift it and holler to Ann, "Come on with the wheel!"

In a whimpering tone she responded, "I can't pick it up."

Another car stopped and the driver asked, "What can I do to help you?"

"If you will bring me the wheel from over there, I'll put it on this trailer," I wearily answered.

The nice man brought the wheel to me and we wired it onto the axle. He was paid in watermelons and Ann and I were "on the road again." After a few miles the wheel again rolled off onto the side of the road. The trailer was pushed into a ditch, and I returned later in the day to take it home.

For Ann, the trip to market was a great adventure. The same afternoon she wrote her mother describing in detail her exciting day. By return mail came a letter from her mother stating, "Your Dad and I didn't work hard all those years to put you through college and have you selling watermelons on the side of the road." As my temper flared, the humor in the letter escaped me, but Ann thought the comment was hilarious.

Selling Electrolux Vacuum Cleaners

To support Ann and me and complete our college degrees, a job was needed to produce an income in addition to the grocery store profits. While working late at Hale's Grocery on a Friday evening, Flois Burroughs, the brother of a high school friend, came by the store.

I asked, "Flois, what are you doing now?"

"Man, I have the best job I've ever had. I sell Electrolux vacuum cleaners," he exclaimed.

He showed me two commission checks, one for $100 and one for $110, he earned in two weeks. I inquired about joining the sales team and Burroughs gave me the manager's name and telephone number. On Monday after calling the Electrolux office an appointment to talk with the manager was arranged.

He asked, "What do you do now, Dub?"

"I am a student at Memphis State College," I responded.

"Oh," he snapped, "we don't hire part-time people."

"Well, I'll assure you of this, if you'll hire me, I'll do more business for you than most of your full-time sales people."

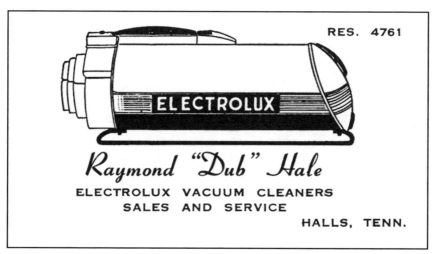

"Dub" Hale began his Electolux sales experience in February 1952, selling in Halls and Memphis, Tennessee. Note the 4-digit telephone number in Halls.

He continued to turn me down for a job even though I used my best persuasion. After several weeks passed I went by the Electrolux office again and met a salesman, Walter Sinks, who was Assistant Manager.

He said, "Dub, I'll put you to work, but don't come to the office when the manager is here because he won't like your being here." I slipped in after hours to pick up vacuum cleaners to sell.

Final exams were in June. Ann and I were married in June and we enjoyed a honeymoon trip to the beach. In June my sales record totaled thirty-seven vacuum cleaners – a busy and successful month. After returning to Memphis the Electrolux Manager was confronted and told I was selling with his company.

He replied, "Yes, I have been reading about you in the *Electrolux News*. You sold thirty seven vacuum cleaners in June – your wedding month. Keep up the good work."

Walter Sinks, my supervisor, told me, "Dub, the company is sponsoring a contest in October encouraging each salesman to sell fifty machines in a month. By meeting the quota, you and Ann will receive an all expense paid trip to the Waldorf-Astoria in New York City."

I exclaimed, "I can't even sell fifty vacuum cleaners in four months. How can I sell fifty in one month?"

"Yes you can," he responded with encouragement.

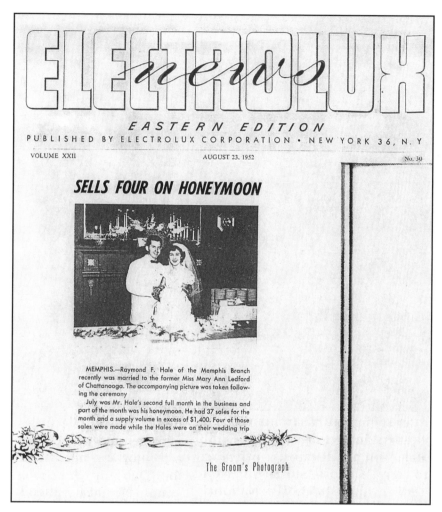

Volume XXII of *Electrolux News*, August 23, 1952, featured "Dub's" record sales of 37 vacuum cleaners in one month.

My competitive spirit surfaced and enthusiasm took control for me to win the contest. The manager's goal of selling fifty vacuum cleaners in a month was reached and Ann and I attended the Electrolux National Convention at the Waldorf-Astoria in April 1953. In the fall of 1953, the company sponsored another

After selling 50 Electrolux vacuum cleaners in October 1952, "Dub" Hale won an all-expense paid trip to the Waldorf-Astoria in New York in April 1953. The National Electrolux Award banquet was a formal occasion attended by Ann and "Dub" with salesmen from across the nation.

Kenny Sinks, Electrolux manager and trainer, was a mentor and best friend to "Dub" in his sales years. He also attended the National Sales Meeting in New York in April, 1953.

contest. The goal was the same – sell fifty vacuum cleaners in a month to win a trip to the Waldorf-Astoria. For the second time the quota was reached and we made the trip to New York City and stayed in the famous hotel in the spring of 1954.

Ann and "Dub" pictured at the Electrolux Awards Banquet in New York City, spring 1954, after he sold another 50 vacuums in one month during the company's 1953 national contest.

My Favorite Electrolux Sales

Three sales are outstanding in my memory of selling vacuum cleaners. My first sale was to a waitress at the restaurant where I worked. After asking the waitress if my sales supervisor, Kenny Sinks, and I could take her home and let him demonstrate the Electrolux vacuum cleaner as a means for me to learn the sales process, she agreed to watch the supervisor's demonstration. He made the sale and gave me the commission which was $40 – twice what I made in the restaurant in a week. On door-to-door calls, Mr. Sinks accompanied me until my sales skills improved. When I became discouraged, he gave me "pep talks."

In a country town like Halls the farmers have money to spend in the fall when the crops are harvested. While making door-to-door calls on a hot, dusty summer afternoon, I stopped by a farmer's home and explained to his wife that I was demonstrating Electrolux vacuum cleaners.

She said, "I wish I had one."

"Where is your husband?" I asked.

She replied, "He is down in the field gathering corn." After driving to the field and watching her husband make a couple of trips through the corn rows, I jumped on the tractor with him.

"I just came from your home and your wife wants me to bring you back to the house to look at something," I told him. He rode with me to his home a mile away.

Carrying my vacuum cleaner in one hand and a box of attachments in the other hand, I stepped into the living room and looked for items to clean. The couple had plastic on the couches and chairs and linoleum on the floors. How could I demonstrate the benefits of all the vacuum attachments with no fabric covered furniture? The floor brush seemed to be the best choice to show the couple the benefits of the machine. While preparing for the demonstration, I looked around the room and asked, "Where is your electrical outlet?"

She quickly responded, "Oh, we don't have electricity."

Amazed, I repeated, "You don't have electricity here?"

"No," she stated.

Through the kitchen door I could see a cooler. I asked, "Is that an icebox or a refrigerator?"

She explained, "That's an icebox, but next month I'll have a new refrigerator delivered. We are getting electricity in a few weeks."

If a good salesman can sell them a refrigerator without electricity, surely I can sell them an Electrolux vacuum cleaner. I demonstrated to the couple the wonderful things the attachments would do when electricity arrived – sweep floors, polish linoleum, dust furniture and paint with a sprayer. Even without electrical outlets the couple was thrilled with their purchase.

At Memphis State marketing and management was a favorite salesmanship class. The teacher knew I sold Electrolux vacuum cleaners after school and thought a demonstration of the machine would be a good program for her class. Following the presentation to the class, my question to her was, "Do you have a vacuum?"

"I do, but it's wearing out," she told me.

That's all I needed to know. "May I come by your home tonight and personally demonstrate to you the amazing things the machine will do, since there is not time in class to show all the machine's features?"

Arriving promptly for the evening appointment and demonstrating the cleaner and attachments with great enthusiasm, I was delighted to sell the machine and accessories. This was a good sale for me, and in addition to a commission, the teacher gave me an "A" in her salesmanship class!

Our Money – in the Stock Market?!?

Our college years were hectic and happy. Ann graduated in 1953 a year ahead of me with a Bachelor of Science degree with a major in Chemistry. She was employed by Proctor and Gamble as a research assistant at a monthly salary of $265 – considerably more than most women earned in 1953.

The first and second months she gave me her paycheck. The third month – no check. After several weeks I questioned what she was doing with her checks since we needed the money for some of our living expenses. Ann confessed to me that a co-worker encouraged her to invest in Proctor and Gamble stock. Not knowing anything about the stock market, I didn't like the idea of investing.

"We're going to lose all of our money!" I declared.

Dub, 1954, and Ann, 1953, graduates of Memphis State College.

Anxiously I watched the stock market quotes in the newspaper daily. Proctor and Gamble stock went from $50 to $55, then $60 and $65 in just a few months.

"You know," I stated, "This looks like an easy way to make money."

As we could afford it, I added to our stock investments. This was my first venture into the stock market. After a positive experience with the market, I began to read and study the "how to" of investments. In 2008, I continue to invest in stocks.

"Off We Go" – into the Air Force

In March 1954, I graduated from Memphis State College with a Bachelor of Science degree in Business

Raymond "Dub" Hale, Jr. pictured third from left, was commissioned a Second Lieutenant in the Air Force by Lt. Col. Rudolf L. Renker at Memphis State College in March 1954.

Administration with a major in Marketing. Having completed the ROTC requirements, I was commissioned a Second Lieutenant in the United States Air Force. In May orders arrived instructing me to report to active duty on June 15, 1954, and I was assigned to the Air Force base in Charleston, South Carolina, for a two year tour of duty.

While in Charleston Ann and I welcomed our first daughter, Susan Duranne, who was born at the military hospital on January 13, 1955. After a five day stay on the maternity ward, Ann and Susan were ready to go home. Expecting all expenses to be paid by the Air

Force, I went to the office to arrange for my family's dismissal from the hospital. There was a balance on my account, but, to my astonishment, the charge was only $9.25. What a difference between maternity and hospital expenses yesterday and today!

"Dub" entered the Air Force in 1954 as a Second Lieutenant after completing the ROTC program at Memphis State College. He reported for duty in Charleston, South Carolina, in June. This family portrait was a Christmas gift to our families at Christmas 1955. Daughter, Susan Duranne, was 11 months old.

Ann and I joined Dorchester-Wayland Baptist Church on arriving in Charleston. A lovely Christian lady, Mrs. Mary Bell, was inspired to start a couple's class of young service people. We were charter members and leaders in developing the class which met in a house beside the church sanctuary. The class grew rapidly to include over twenty-five couples and a larger space was needed to accommodate the growing membership. For us, two years in the Air Force passed quickly and the time had come to leave the people and places we had grown to love.

While in Charleston, South Carolina, we enjoyed the "Old South" by touring the beautiful gardens, visiting the Battery Place overlooking Fort Sumter where the first shots of the Civil War were fired, and enjoying the lovely beaches of Foley Island and Mount Pleasant.

Ann and I were at a crossroads in our lives as we prepared to leave the Air Force. Should we return to Memphis and buy a grocery store or move to Chattanooga and pursue a new career – the choice would shape our destiny. On June 14, 1956, I was discharged from the Air Force. We chose Chattanooga since we felt there were more opportunities and the location was near her family.

Chapter 9
CHOOSING A CAREER

A New Career in Real Estate

Charles A. Fike, Ann's uncle, was a successful real estate broker/owner in Chattanooga. He invited me to join his firm, Fike Realty, as a real estate agent and insurance salesman – both strictly on commission. After accepting his offer I was eager to start my new career. Although Mr. Fike welcomed me, his office was filled with real estate agents and he informed me he didn't have a desk for me. There was a solution to the dilemma. A storage room of signs and discarded items could be an office if I wanted to clear, paint and furnish it. I accepted the challenge.

On the Fourth of July 1956, Ann's dad, Mr. Ledford, and I cleaned and painted the room then looked in the newspaper under "used furniture" to select furnishings for my new office. A gentleman advertised a big oak desk and chair for $35. At my request he held the furniture until morning when Mr. Ledford and I loaded the new purchases on his truck and hurried to our destination – my newly renovated office in the Professional Building on Georgia Avenue.

Working diligently for over two months to make a sale, I became discouraged when it didn't happen. In an effort to generate an income for my family and in desperation, I checked out six Electrolux vacuum cleaners and began "knocking doors" once again. My business card advertised "real estate, insurance and vacuum cleaners" – whatever one needed.

While canvassing the neighborhood to sell vacuum cleaners and insurance, a man referred me to a friend who needed insurance on his home. After selling him and his brother, who lived next door, policies for their homes and contents I felt re-energized at the prospect of making a living in sales. These sales re-

---

FIKE REALTY COMPANY
REAL ESTATE - LOANS
PHONE 2-2102 OR 7-3886

HALE & FIKE GENERAL INSURANCE
FIRE, CASUALTY, AUTO, LIFE
PHONE 2-2102 OR 7-3886

ELECTROLUX
BONDED REPRESENTATIVE
ELECTROLUX CLEANERS, SALES & SERVICE
PHONE 2-2102 OR 2-3884

RAYMOND "DUB" HALE, JR.
6909 GREENWAY DRIVE

Raymond "Dub" Hale joined Fike Realty Company in July 1956 representing the real estate and insurance businesses. Selling Electrolux vacuum cleaners "door-to-door" gave him extra income and many contacts in the community. This business card says it all!

minded me that "seeing the people face-to-face" and getting "referrals" generate leads that are productive.

With renewed energy and enthusiasm, I started "knocking doors" in East Ridge to sell my cleaners. When a lady responded my greeting was, "I'm Raymond Hale with Electrolux."

To my astonishment, she said, "Bring it on in."

I had just begun my Electrolux demonstration complete with attachments when she remarked, "that's the one I want." Being delighted with the speedy sale the contract was quickly signed.

When leaving I asked the lady, "Have you seen the machine before today?"

"Yes," she said, "a salesman was here and demonstrated the cleaner last week, but I didn't buy it. This morning I called the office and asked for one to be delivered."

This was the easiest sale I ever made – my lucky day!

Walking to my car I noticed the house across the street was over-grown with grass and weeds and a "for-sale-by-owner" sign was in the yard. No one was home, but I left a business card in the door. That evening a call came from the owner who was getting a divorce and selling his house. When the home was inspected, the only remaining furniture was a bed, chair, table and television. His wife had returned in his absence and taken the furniture. His remaining possessions were hidden in the attic – just in case she returned unexpectedly.

To get the house in marketable condition, I cut the grass and freshened the house with paint. The owner listed the property with me, and a Fike Realty sign was placed in the yard.

The Labor Day weekend was near and brought my first real estate sale. Ann and I had invited friends for a holiday cookout, and as we were heating the grill, a call came to show the "just listed" house. My friend accompanied me and we drove to the property, met the prospect and showed the house. I sold it!

After struggling for three months to find my place in the Chattanooga sales market, this first sale set my real estate career in a positive direction to a successful, life-long profession.

Trading Homes In Real Estate

While working at Fike Realty, I developed a system to help buyers trade their used home on a new home as they "moved up" in home ownership. Sales were often contingent on selling the home the buyers owned before they could buy the home of their dreams. In my first experience at trading, the first four contracts depended on selling the fifth home. Mr. Fike and I bought the fifth home or took it in on "trade," in the chain of sales to make the four sales close. Four commissions were paid when the sales closed and the house we "traded" sold quickly to make my fifth sale. The success of these "domino" sales inspired Mr. Fike and me to expand our horizons on selling opportunities. "Trading houses" became our market "niche."

The leading caption on my advertising became "Will Trade." To be a trader you had to know the value of the home the buyer owned to be accurate with the allowance on the new home. Most salesmen did not want to take that kind of risk. When they received calls to "trade" on a home, they referred the calls to me. "Trading" was a new, innovative way of doing real estate business and became my trademark. By now I knew moving to Chattanooga and going into the real estate business was the best decision for our family.

903 Woodmore Terrace was built in 1957.

Our second daughter, Linda Joan Hale, arrived on September 12, 1957. Six weeks later Ann and I moved into a new home we designed and built at 905 Woodmore Terrace in the Woodmore community of North Brainerd.

Carrie Comes to Clean and Care

As my real estate business increased and just before our second baby was expected, Ann and I needed help at home with our family and housekeeping responsibilities. Carrie Davenport, who worked for the Ledfords, agreed to work for us one day a week. Susan was nineteen months old in August 1957 when Carrie began her journey through life's adventures with the Hales. Joan was born in September and Dianne two and one-half years later. Our family was complete.

Ann and I were involved in political, community and church activities and often entertained family and friends at dinner parties and picnics. With three small children and busy schedules we needed additional help with our home and daughters. In 1961 we employed Carrie five days a week. She was a positive influence on our children as she helped care for them, disciplined them and loved them. She was with the family through the children's school days, college years, marriages and births of their children. She helped Susan, Joan and Dianne build memories to cherish a lifetime.

Carrie worked with our family for forty-seven years until her retirement on December 31, 2004, to have some years of rest and leisure and to care for her mother.

Carrie Davenport and Ann celebrate at Ann's 70th birthday party.

Hale Realty is Established

With a new home and a new baby, Linda Joan, I established a new real estate office – HALE REALTY. On January 1, 1958, the doors of Hale Realty opened to new challenges and opportunities never imagined. One salesman, Ernest Palmer, and a part-time secretary completed my staff.

The office at 1020 McCallie Avenue was a house purchased for $6000 and renovated into offices. Hale Realty occupied the first floor and on the second floor were four rooms that were later remodeled into offices and rented for $25 a month. My savings of $4000 was spent on remodeling the building and no additional funds were available to pave the parking lot.

My father-in-law, Mr. Ledford, occasionally came by for a visit and always asked, "When are your going to pave your parking lot?"

I always answered, "Oh, I'm going to fix it next week." Next week never came because there was no extra money to finish the work. Mr. Ledford realized the problem, so he offered to loan me $4000 to complete the parking lot. This was the only occasion money was borrowed from my father-in-law.

Hale Realty's first office building was a home at 1020 McCallie Avenue which was remodeled and occupied in 1958. (Building on the right.) Later the house next door (1022) was purchased, renovated and used as rental property.

A year after successfully opening and operating Hale Realty, I invited my brother Bob, who was working at a grocery store in Memphis, to come work with me. Together we opened Hale Insurance Company which he managed.

In December 1959 Mother and Dad called to tell me they had sold Hale's Grocery and planned to move to Chattanooga to be with Bob, Ann, the grandchildren and me. This decision brought all my family together again. Soon after their arrival in Chattanooga, our third daughter, Edith Dianne Hale, was born on April 23, 1960. Six months later we built a new home at 1222 Collins Circle where we lived for ten years.

The Hales moved to 1222 Collins Circle in 1960.

Dad knew a little about construction. We purchased three lots and he built several small houses. In 1962, after being in the real estate business for several years and with the help of Dad and Bob, I ventured into the home building business. The dilemma was how to get started building houses without adequate financing.

Ralph Chumley, a friend and loan officer with Chamberlain Mortgage Company, who assisted me with loans for my home buyers and previous construction, advised me to consult several land developers before entering the home building business.

Waverly Park, a subdivision in North Georgia near Lake Winnepesaukah Amusement Park, was being developed by Smith and Wood Construction Company. After consulting with them, I purchased thirty lots to begin the home building division of Hale Realty. Dad was doing well in construction and my brother Bob was looking forward to joining him to build houses in Waverly Park.

Ralph Chumley loaned me construction money. Dad and Bob built the houses. Hale Realty sold them – and I took a "trade," if necessary. This business arrangement was a win/win/win situation for all of us. Sadly, Dad passed away in August 1964.

Our success in Waverly Park inspired me to expand my home building skills to a larger subdivision. Ralph Chumley recommended me to Meredith Foster, a land developer in Catoosa County, Georgia, who owned the Morris Estates subdivision. Foster allowed me to buy lots and pay for them after selling the houses. In 1965 a partnership was formed with Garnet Forrester, a North Georgia developer, to build two-hundred homes over ten years in Morris Estates. Three streets in the subdivision were named for our daughters, Susan Road, Joan Drive and Dianne Lane. Susan and Dianne

HOMES BUILT with BRICK
for good LIVING

10 NEW BRICK HOMES... BUILDERS... UNITED BUILDERS, Coy Riddle, Smith and Wood... DON'T MISS SEEING

ALL BRICK HOMES

- GI—NOTHING DOWN
- CONVENTIONAL 10% DOWN
- LIVING ROOM

- GARAGE or CARPORT
- FHA—$450 DOWN
- 3-BEDROOM
- DINING AREA OR FAMILY ROOM

- $84-$96 A MONTH
- 1½ CERAMIC BATHS
- PAVED DRIVEWAYS PATIOS AT SOME

HOW TO GET THERE

RINGGOLD RD.

MISSIONARY RIDGE

McBRIEN

LAKEVIEW DR.

CROSS

Lake Winnepesaukah

LAKEVIEW HIGH S.   WAVERLY PARK

AGENTS:

★ Hale Realty, Phone 266-5681
★ Tenn. Valley Realty, Phone 622-1520

General Shale
Products Corp.

August 11, 1963

Waverly Park

Looking over plans for Morris Estates subdivision are Ralph Chumley, manager Murphree Mortgage Company, and Raymond and Bob Hale, Hale Realty.

Morris Estates was Raymond Hale's largest and most successful subdivision development.

lament the fact their streets were platted on the subdivision map but never constructed. Joan Drive remains a popular address in Morris Estates. This was my largest and most successful subdivision development.

While working in Morris Estates, construction was begun on houses in Poplar Springs, a nearby subdivision. Over fifty homes were built before moving our construction crew to a site in Tennessee.

Lakebrook, a Tennessee subdivision near Shallowford Road, was my next development. Since Mother

Lakebrook

was now alone, I built her a home in Lakebrook where she enjoyed her six granddaughters until her death on January 1, 1973.

Raymond and Ann's daughters and nieces celebrate at a family gathering on Christmas Eve 1971. Gathering around the tree are Raymond and Bob's children, Jo, Lee, Dianne, Joan, Lori and Susan.

Over the next few years forty-five homes were completed in the subdivision before I returned to North Georgia to continue home building in Plemons Estates in 1984.

Sundays were busy days for our family. We went to Sunday School and church at Central Baptist Church, Woodmore. After hurrying home for a sandwich, I arrived at the subdivision by 1 P.M. and prospective buyers toured the homes until 6 P.M. Sunday nights were filled with youth activities for the children, Finance and Deacon Committee meetings and a worship service.

With a trade program, easy financing, a good builder, and a successful marketing program, Hale Realty was growing and expanding. The offices on McCallie Avenue became crowded as the company grew.

The north Georgia subdivision of Plemons Estates was developed in 1984 by Raymond Hale. Attending the grand opening are (in front) Jim Hall, Senior Vice President of First Tennessee Bank and manager of the Commercial Banking Department, and wife Ina Hall. (In back) Susan Hale Chastain, Hale Realty office manager; Mitch Chastain, builder; Meredith Foster, developer; Raymond Hale, Hale Realty.

The Dale Carnegie Course

As a part of training in my sales career, I enrolled in the Dale Carnegie Course taught by Sherman Paul who was an expert on developing young men to be leaders. Paul gave his students opportunities to practice speaking confidently and spontaneously. Remembering names and faces is a necessary skill in sales. The students learned techniques to retain in memory names of customers and clients. The Dale Carnegie Course impressed and inspired me to sponsor six of my Hale Realty agents to attend the classes and benefit from the education.

Bill McLaughlin Joins Hale Realty

Bill McLaughlin joined me at Hale Realty in August 1961 after completing a tour of duty in the Army. Bill is the bright-eyed, personable ten year old who worked at Hale's Grocery in the 1940's. When he entered junior high school he lived with my parents, Raymond and Pauline, for two years and helped in the store while I was away at college.

Bill graduated from Halls High School with honors and awards. He was chosen by the American Legion Post to attend a week-long all expense paid trip to Boys State to learn about state government.

After graduating from high school, Bill was offered a football scholarship to Murray State College. He could not accept the partial scholarship because

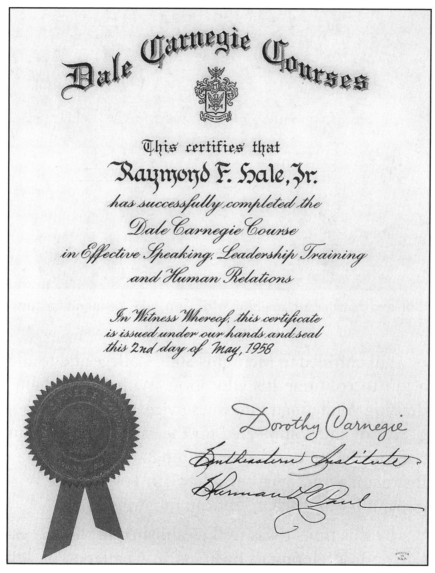

Dale Carnegie Courses

This certifies that

Raymond F. Hale, Jr.

has successfully completed the

Dale Carnegie Course

in Effective Speaking, Leadership Training

and Human Relations

In Witness Whereof, this certificate
is issued under our hands and seal
this 2nd day of May, 1958

Dorothy Carnegie

Southeastern Institute

Herman L. Paul

Raymond Hale's certificate of graduation from the Dale Carnegie Course in effective speaking, leadership training and human relations

there were no additional funds for expenses. The time had come to leave Hale's Grocery where he was employed for almost ten years. It was a sad "good bye".

Bill and Martha McLaughlin with Ann and Raymond in June 2002

Bill enrolled in Memphis State College and found a job to continue his education. With "Uncle Sam" drafting young men into the service, Bill dropped out of school and volunteered for the Army to choose his path in the military. After training and serving as an instructor at an aviation school in Fort Eustice, Virginia, Bill was discharged from the Army in 1961.

By this time, I was well established in the real estate and development business in Chattanooga. Bill was invited to join Hale Realty and learn the real estate business. He gladly accepted my offer and began his real estate career in August 1961. One year later he married Martha Clayton, a high school classmate. Martha taught school until the adoption of their son Scot. One year later a daughter Kim was born.

Five years after coming to Chattanooga, Interstate Life and Accident Insurance Company offered Bill a job in the real estate department. This afforded him the opportunity to work and go to school in the evenings on the G. I. Bill of Rights. Bill completed his college work and received a Bachelor of Science degree in Business Administration from the University of Tennessee at Chattanooga.

Both Bill and Martha have families in West Tennessee, so they decided to move to Memphis in late 1972 where Bill entered the mortgage and banking business. In 1980, he joined Union Planters Bank as vice-president and was promoted to Senior Vice President and Senior Real Estate Credit Officer for Union Planters Corporation where he worked until his retirement in January 2007.

Bill's journey to success was a trip of commitment and determination to receive an education and to find a career that maximized his talents. After struggling to complete high school, working at Hale's Grocery, serving in the Army, learning the real estate business at Hale Realty, graduating from college, having a family and a productive banking career, Bill has reached the pinnacle of his "mountain climb" to success. He and Martha are enjoying "peace in the valley" after their ascent on the mountain. Their Christian faith has sustained them every step of the way.

Bill is like a brother to me and we have kept in touch through the years.

Ledford's Service Station Is Sold

For over forty years Mr. and Mrs. Ledford, Ann's parents, owned and operated Ledford's Service Station at 3424 Brainerd Road. The Brainerd community where the Ledfords lived and worked was a prosperous, growing community in the 1940's and 1950's and a variety of businesses emerged to serve the growing area. Mr. Ledford's "full service" station employed attendants who

C. Durand and Edith Ledford, Ann's parents

pumped gas, cleaned windshields and checked air pressure in the tires when customers stopped by. "Full Service" included tire sales and repairs, oil changes, road service, and washing and polishing cars until they sparkled.

Those were the days when you requested your automobile to be picked up at home, serviced and returned. Mr. Ledford cared about his customers, took good care of their cars and developed friendships that lasted a lifetime. Mrs. Ledford helped at the service station by answering the phone, setting service appointments, and collecting the accounts.

Carl's Restaurant at Brainerd Road was the location of the first Kentucky Fried Chicken franchise in Chattanooga. Raymond sold the adjoining property, Ledford's Service Station, to Carl Martin to be demolished for additional parking in October 1966. Pictured: Carl Martin, Colonel Sanders (cut out) and Raymond Hale.

In January, 1966, just before turning sixty-five years of age, Mr. Ledford retired and sold his station. Located next to Ledford's Service Station was the first Kentucky Fried Chicken franchised restaurant in Chattanooga, owned by Carl Martin.

The service station was sold to Martin who demolished it to make additional parking for his fast growing restaurant business.

Mr. Ledford was assisted by me in the sale of his station and the transition to retirement.

$300,000 Office Building Project Set for Brainerd

THIS ARTIST'S DRAWING SHOWS HOW THE NEW HALE BUILDING AT 3503 BRAINERD RD. WILL LOOK WHEN IT IS ERECTED

By FRED SCHNEIDER

Plans for a $300,000 office building development at 3503 Brainerd Rd. were announced Saturday by Raymond F. Hale Jr., realtor and head of the R. F. Hale Realty firm.

To be known as the Hale Building, its first unit will be started within two weeks and then in about a year a second building will be started. The first unit will contain 10,000 square feet and the second 5,000 square feet.

Site for the development was purchased from Lovemans Inc. It forms an "L" extending to Tunnel Boulevard. The property fronts 122 feet on Brainerd Road has a maximum depth of 316 feet and then extends 279 feet to Tunnel Boulevard fronting 70 feet on that street.

The first building will be a two-story structure facing Brainerd Road with both floors at ground level because of the contour of the lot and will have entrances from both Brainerd Road and Tunnel Boulevard.

The second building will be one story in height facing Tunnel Boulevard. There is a brick residence on this section of the property which will remain until time for the next phase of construction.

Chapter 10
EXPANDING IN BUSINESS

A New Home For Hale Realty

After purchasing a tract of ground at 3505 Brainerd Road, my first office complex was built with over 10,000 square feet of floor space. The Hale Building, designed by architects Bianculli and Tyler, displayed the most modern design and construction in the area. Hale Realty moved into the front office of the new building and the remaining offices were leased.

THE HALE BUILDING with over 10,000 square feet of floor space was the first phase of the office development at 3505 Brainerd Road planned by Raymond Hale. It was Chattanooga's newest and most modern office building.

February 10, 1967, was the date chosen to celebrate the dedication and ribbon cutting for the new Hale Building at 3505 Brainerd Road. County Judge Chester Frost and Chattanooga Mayor
Ralph Kelley did the honors of cutting the ribbon. Surrounding
them were The Reverend Ansell T. Baker, Pastor of Central Baptist
Church; Jack Tyler and Harvey Camp, Architects; Raymond Hale,
owner of Hale Realty; Elgin Smith, Elgin Smith Realtors, Inc.,
President of the Chattanooga Association of REALTORS.

City and County officials joined our family for the
ribbon-cutting and dedication ceremony of the Hale
Building on February 10, 1967. Family, friends and
dignitaries attended the celebration.

On the remaining land at the rear of the Hale
Building the Hale Apartments were constructed and
quickly filled with tenants.

Two years later a lot on the corner of Brainerd Road
and Tunnel Boulevard became available for purchase.

Agents and staff on Dedication day for the new Hale Building

An office building of 15,000 square feet built on this tract of land was my next project. After ten months under construction the Michael Building was occupied by J. B. Michael Construction Company. Bruce Gilpatrick who managed the company became a good friend and later a real estate agent with Hale Realty.

Raymond Hale's family joined him to celebrate the opening of the new office building at 3505 Brainerd Road. Gathered around him are his daughters, Dianne, Susan and Joan. Standing are his wife, Ann,; mother, Pauline Hale,; brother, Bob; and mother and father-in-law, Edith and C.D. Ledford.

Tom and Tim – My Faithful Helpers

With the responsibility of over thirty-three thousand square feet of office space to maintain, I employed two young men, Tom Phillips and Tim Johnson, to help me keep the buildings in good shape for the tenants.

On Tunnel Boulevard across from the Hale Realty office building, Tom Phillips lived with his mother. Tom was the youngest of eight children and the only one remaining at home. His father passed away when he was young leaving his mother to provide for the family by working at the hospital.

Tom was in the seventh grade when I offered him the opportunity to work with me on Saturdays. Being delighted to make extra money to help him in school he arrived promptly at 7 A.M. on Saturday to work diligently through the day. He emptied wastebaskets, assisted me in changing filters and replacing fluorescent bulbs for lighting the offices. The paycheck helped Tom with expenses and provided a few dollars to save. His goal of a higher education seemed far, far away, but he continued to dream of college.

After high school graduation Tom enrolled at the University of Tennessee at Chattanooga and graduated with a degree in Criminal Justice. Tom, his wife Christy and three sons live in Dalton, Georgia, where he is employed by the Dalton Police Department and enjoys an outstanding career in law enforcement.

When Tom Phillips entered the University, I selected as my helper another bright, energetic young man,

Tim Johnson, Raymond's "faithful helper"

Tim Johnson, who is the son of our long-time friends James and Martha Johnson. Since Tim lived in our neighborhood, giving him a ride to the office was a convenient arrangement. On Saturday mornings Tim was ready for work and looking out the window awaiting my 6 o'clock arrival. We always stopped for a breakfast of bacon, sausage, pancakes and juice. A big breakfast started the day because we worked until 3 P.M.

Tim was my faithful helper through his high school years. Choosing Covenant College for his higher education, he graduated with a Bachelor of Science degree in Business Administration. In the early 1980's Tim was certified by the state of Tennessee as an Emergency Medical Technician (EMT). While working with the Tri-Community Fire and Ambulance Service, he received the prestigious Officer of the Year Award on two occasions.

Tim, his wife Cindy and two daughters, Jessica and Ashley reside in Collegedale, Tennessee, where he is a member of the City Commission and has served as Vice Mayor and Mayor. He is employed by Cigna Health Care as Account Manager, National Accounts.

Having two wonderful, Christian young men, Tom and Tim, work with me in their teenage years was a privilege. With commitment and diligence, their goals of achieving college degrees were reached. Providing work and encouraging Tom and Tim toward their goals gave me a great sense of pride.

President of the Chattanooga Association of REALTORS

At the new location, the Hale Building at 3505 Brainerd Road, companies in addition to Hale Realty were developed including Hale Insurance Company,

Hale Mortgage Company and United Builders, a construction company.

Along with business commitments, time and energy were volunteered for the advancement of the real estate industry. As a result of involvement in the Chattanooga Association of REALTORS, the trade group elected and installed me as 1968 President.

The following year the Association honored me with the prestigious "REALTOR of the Year" award for service to the organization.

Mrs. Ruth Faris, chairman of the REALTOR of the Year Committee of the Chattanooga Board of REALTORS, presents an engraved plaque to Raymond F. Hale, at right, designating him Chattanooga's "REALTOR of the Year" for 1969. Bill Clift, C.E. Clift Realty, president of the Chattanooga Board of REALTORS, observes the presentation on May 14, 1969.

Hamilton County Baptist Association

In addition to our business, community and church activities, Ann and I have been involved in the ministries of the Hamilton County Baptist Association. As we extended our involvement from our local church to the wider area of service through the Association, we served on committees and in positions of leadership under the Director of Missions, Dr. J. V. James. For several years I served as Treasurer of the Association and Ann was Director of the Woman's Missionary Union (WMU).

When I sold my two office buildings on McCallie Avenue, the Baptist leaders purchased them to relocate the Hamilton County Baptist Association offices. As the Baptist work expanded the office buildings were sold and the HCBA offices were moved to North Chattanooga. When a new office building was constructed for the Hamilton County Baptist Association at 508 North Market Street, in the heart of the North Shore, I served as chairman of the Building Committee. My responsibilities were to assist in developing the plans and arranging for financing of the new building.

God's vision was outstanding in selecting and guiding the leaders to the location for the new offices. After prayer and planning, the construction began at the North Market Street site. Although the area was not progressive at the time, it was a central location the Association could afford.

Following the retirement of Dr. J. V. James, Dr. David Al Myers and wife Brenda came to Chattanooga at the invitation of the Association Search Committee of which Ann was a member. Dr. Myers became Director of Missions in the late 1970's and has served over twenty-five years with the Hamilton County Baptist Association.

Under Dr. Myer's direction, the Association sponsors inner-city camps, multi-cultural churches, and Hocoba, a food and clothing outlet for the less fortunate in the community. He continues to provide progressive and inspirational leadership among the Baptist churches and in the religious community.

Looking over the budget for the Hamilton County Baptist Association in October 1969 are moderator, The Reverend Duane Highlander (Pastor, Middle Valley Baptist); vice-moderator, The Reverend Ben L. Peacock (Pastor, East Lake Baptist); clerk, Mrs. Claude A . Park, Jr.; treasurer, Raymond F. Hale, Jr. (Central Baptist); superintendent of missions, The Reverend J. V. James.

As years have passed the North Shore has come alive through the vision of our city and county leaders and developers. The "Four Bridges" – the renovated Market Street Bridge, Olgiati Bridge, Veterans' Bridge with American flags flying, and historic pedestrian Walnut Street Bridge – give easy access from downtown Chattanooga to the North Shore.

Coolidge and Renaissance Parks are "green" areas in the fast developing river front community. New high-rise condos and town homes define the skyline. Exclusive neighborhoods are blending with historic cottage homes of the 1920's and 1930's to provide a variety of housing. The Theatre Centre, upscale restaurants and boutique shops give character to the redevelopment of the original "Hill City".

The Hamilton County Baptist Association is now in the center of Chattanooga's redevelopment and stands as a testimony to the faith and commitment of Baptist leaders to plant a Christian witness in the "heart of Chattanooga."

President of Woodmore Elementary School PTA

In the 1960's the Woodmore Elementary School was a new, progressive school a few blocks from our home in the North Brainerd community of Woodmore. Principal Claude Johnson supervised an efficient office staff and an outstanding group of teachers dedicated to excellence in education. In the area schools there was a spirit of cooperation and camaraderie by the parents in supporting the goals of the Principal and teachers through the Parent Teacher Association.

In the early 1970's the Woodmore Parent Teacher Association needed leadership for the coming year. My friend and next door neighbor, Keith Wilson, was Chairman of the nominating committee to select leaders for the 1971-72 year.

Keith called one evening and asked to visit me. I said, "Sure, Keith, come on over." The object of his call was to enlist me as President of the PTA.

I responded, "Keith, I am too busy to say 'yes' to any more jobs. I have my family and business responsibilities and I can't accept the PTA presidency at this time, but thanks for considering me."

Keith was very persuasive saying, "Raymond, our nominating committee unanimously agrees you should lead the PTA in the coming school year."

"How many people have you asked to take this job?," I inquired.

"Only three," Keith replied.

His desperation in finding a leader gave me a guilty feeling about saying, "No." I felt the "call to duty" and accepted the challenge of the PTA presidency for 1971-72.

Summer planning meetings with a lively exchange of ideas led the PTA Board of Directors to select an ambitious project for the coming year – air conditioning classrooms at Woodmore Elementary School. In the 1960's and 1970's, only the breezes through open windows determined the temperature in the rooms. The hot, sweltering days of early fall and late spring made the classrooms uncomfortable and the children anxious for the school year to end.

The PTA membership gave permission to buy and install the air conditioners. The Board of Education and Superintendent of Schools, Jim Henry, furnished the electricians for the installation. As news traveled about this tremendous undertaking to air condition the school, parents, teachers and students were enthusiastic about improving the school facilities. The first PTA meeting of my presidency drew an unprecedented crowd of over five hundred parents and teachers to the school auditorium. Since there was no air conditioning and the windows were open, some attendees stood on the outside of the auditorium looking in through the windows – anxious to be a part of making the school "cool before spring."

As PTA President "mobilizing the troops" to raise over $12,000 for purchase and installation of air conditioners was a challenge. Fund-raising projects included sales of Krispy-Kreme donuts, baked goods, candy bars and Christmas wrapping paper. A carnival and chili supper were enjoyed by the neighborhood and, of course, generous donations were accepted.

By mid-winter the funds were available to begin the work. Principal Claude Johnson, dads and volunteer technicians worked long and hard on evenings and weekends to have the school cool by the warm days of spring. The children enjoyed the comfortable classrooms in April and May.

The news came in the summer months of 1972 that many of the children, including our youngest daughter Dianne, would be bussed to a distant school in the fall. Enjoying the cool rooms was a short lived pleasure, as the children were relocated to schools in other communities or were enrolled in private schools. The schools and community were forever changed as new children and families moved into the Woodmore area.

President of Tennessee Association of REALTORS

The Tennessee Association of REALTORS installed me as President in June 1972. Meeting with Governor Winfield Dunn was a privilege when I represented the Tennessee Association of REALTORS in promoting National REALTORS Week. Governor Dunn signed a Proclamation recognizing the professional services of REALTORS and their contributions made to the real estate industry.

In November of that year the national convention was in Honolulu, Hawaii. Ann and I had reservations at the Penthouse of Hilton's Rainbow Tower overlooking Waikiki Beach and Diamondhead. A trip to paradise island was the thrill of a lifetime.

Tennessee Governor Winfield Dunn joined the officers of the Tennessee Association of REALTORS to sign a proclamation for National REALTORS week. Pictured in the spring of 1972 with Governor Dunn are Carl Storey of Nashville, Vice President; Charles Faris of Chattanooga, Secretary-Treasurer; and Raymond Hale, President.

Touring the Islands gave us an insight into the beauty and diverse culture of our fiftieth state. As I looked over the white, sandy beaches on the beautiful island of Oahu, I reflected on my early beginnings and thought, "It's A Long Way From Halls!"

As President of the Tennessee REALTORS, the responsibility was mine to interview candidates for an assistant to the Executive Officer. Steve Harding applied for the position and stood out in the crowd of potential staff members. Steve was hired by the Association in late 1973 and served the professional group, first as Assistant to the Executive Officer and later, as Executive Vice President – a position he holds today.

Linda Woods came to the Association as Secretary five years prior to Steve's arrival. She has worked with Steve through the years as the TAR membership has grown from 5,160 in the early 1970's to 27,000 in 2008. As Administrative Vice President, Linda coordinates the many responsibilities of the Association, including the meetings and conventions.

Steve and Linda have guided the Tennessee Association of REALTORS to an outstanding and prestigious position in the National Association of REALTORS.

Linda Woods, Administrative Vice President, and Steve Harding, Executive Vice President of the Tennessee Association of REALTORS join Raymond and Ann Hale at the TAR convention in Chattanooga in 2008.

They made my presidency, which extended from June 1972 through December 1973, a wonderful experience.

In June 1973, as President of the Tennessee Association of REALTORS, I presided over the state convention in Chattanooga, Tennessee. J. D. Sawyer, pres-

Forrest Cate, Jr., owner of Forrest Cate Ford, was the featured speaker at the Tennessee Association of REALTORS prayer breakfast at the Read House in June 1973. Cate, who had been blind for several years, gave an inspirational message accompanied by his "service dog" Romulus. Pictured with the speaker are J.D. Sawyer, President of the National Association of REALTORS; Bob Land, President Elect of the Chattanooga Association of REALTORS; Raymond Hale, President of the Tennessee Association of REALTORS; Forrest Cate, Jr. with Romulus; and Hugh Siniard, President of the Chattanooga Association of REALTORS.

ident of the National Association of REALTORS, was an honored guest at the meeting. A spirit of optimism filled the room as he projected growth in the economy and home sales over the next two years.

Forrest Cate, Jr., owner of Forrest Cate Ford, was the inspirational speaker at a breakfast meeting. His story of overcoming difficulties in life as he lost his vision was an emotional testimony to God's goodness and guidance in stressful times.

Romulus, his service guide dog, laid very still and quiet at his feet as Cate spoke. The dog knew the speech as well as the speaker. As Cate approached the end of his comments, Romulus raised his head, thumped his tail loudly on the floor and prepared to leave the room. Amid generous applause, Realtors said "good bye" to a distinguished Christian gentleman, Forrest Cate, Jr., and his best friend Romulus.

After enjoying the National Convention in Hawaii the previous year, the Hawaiian theme was carried over to the State convention. A buffet dinner and luau at Lakeshore Lodge overlooking the Tennessee River was the highlight of the convention meeting. Susan, Joan and Dianne, our daughters, joined Ann and me for the festive occasion.

The "Tennessee Realtor" magazine communicated the state news to all Realtors and as president an article was contributed by me each month. Featured in the Christmas issue was our family portrait which accompanied "The President's Message."

Raymond serving as Tennessee Association of REALTORS president, presided over the State Convention in Chattanooga in 1973. The family is pictured at a luau at Lakeshore Resort. Raymond Hale; daughters Joan, Dianne and Susan; Ann Hale.

Family portrait in *Tennesse Realtor* magazine, December, 1973

Surviving a Hurricane in Mexico

In June 1974 the Tennessee Association of REAL-TORS convention was in Acapulco, Mexico, where four planes landed with five hundred enthusiastic Tennessee Realtors. As convention chairman I felt responsible for the group and the travel arrangements. After a few days on the beautiful, sunny beaches of Mexico, time had come to fly home.

As we enjoyed breakfast on the morning of departure, dark clouds hovered over the ocean and hotel. Our waitress knew we were leaving that day and commented with assurance in broken English, "Planes no fly today." Ann and I assured her the planes would fly because four planes awaited the Realtors at the airport a few miles away.

The Realtors rode in a driving rain to the airport on chartered buses. When we reached the airport we were told the worst hurricane in Acapulco history was sweeping the area and washing away homes and streets. The first plane destined for Memphis was signaled to depart, but the remaining three flights were cancelled.

After communicating with the Mexican airport officials throughout the day about arrangements for our departure, suddenly no one spoke English – a terrible inconvenience. All the luggage was setting on carts on the tarmac with no one making an effort to rescue it. Rain was coming through the roof. Travelers were getting ill from drinking the water and eating the food.

After staying in the airport over seven hours, the chartered buses returned to provide transportation back to the hotel. Taking off our shoes and rolling up our slacks, we waded in knee-deep water to board the buses. The drivers were herding the Realtors onto the buses as quickly as possible before the water was too deep for them to roll. As we drove over back roads through the mountains high above Acapulco, huge rocks were plummeting down on the bus and the road was washing away behind us. We were praying for a safe return to the city.

Our luggage remained at the airport, so we had only the clothes on our backs for sleeping and wearing on our trip home. The following day the skies were blue and sunny as we rode to the airport, but the group could see the poverty and destruction left by the hurricane in the rural areas of Mexico. The plane departed on schedule, and a cheer of relief sounded from the Realtors as the wheels left the runway.

Our daughters, Susan, Joan, and Dianne were with us on the trip. Ann and I thought the opportunity for them to travel to another country was a great educational experience. However, at that point, we vowed never again to have the family traveling together on one plane. The risk of losing all our family at one time is just too great.

Following my service as President of the Tennessee Association of REALTORS, the organization honored me as "1974 Tennessee REALTOR of the Year." At the

National Convention in Las Vegas, Nevada, President Joe Daughtery presented each state honoree with an engraved silver revere bowl in recognition of commitment to Realtor excellence.

In Las Vegas, Nevada, at the National Convention, Raymond F. Hale is congratulated by Joseph B. Doherty, president of the National Association of REALTORS, on his selection as 1974 Tennessee REALTOR of the Year.

After several years of service in the real estate industry, I was twice elected a Director of the National Association of REALTORS holding the position in 1972-1978 and 1984-1987.

Chapter 11
FAMILY ADVENTURES

And the Floods Came

Ann and I and our three daughters lived at 4319 Shawhan Road in the Woodmore community in the Spring of 1973 when flood waters covered much of Chattanooga. The season was rainy from the previous November through March and the grounds were saturated with water. When the Spring rains persisted, the

The massive flood of March 1973 damaged the Ledford and Hale homes on Shawhan Road.

area suffered one of the worst floods in the city's history.

As waters rose in the creek behind our home, police with bullhorns drove through the neigh-borhood urging people to evacuate the area. Ann and I alerted her parents who lived next door. We packed three cars with food, blankets, family and a pet to take us to a safe place in my offices at Hale Realty on Brain-erd Road.

Albert and Alice Waller invited our family to stay with them until the flood waters receded.

After my family was safe, Ann and I drove through the community to assist others attempting to get their possessions to higher ground.

Four feet of water stood in our home for several days and the clean-up was a massive task. Our cousins, Alice and Albert Waller, invited the Ledfords and our family to stay with them until we could return to our homes.

A sense of humor helps one through difficult times. Mr. Ledford, Ann's Dad, kept extra cash and savings in a safe in his basement. The flood waters soaked every-thing including his money. After the flood waters re-ceded and we returned home, I went next door to see

Mr. Ledford. Walking into the house I smelled something burning in the kitchen. Mr. Ledford was attempting to rescue his singed money from the oven where he was trying to dry it. Needless to say, that wasn't a good idea – but the bank did replace his currency.

Vacations at Daytona Beach, Florida

The Allen Jordan family accompanied the Hale family on a beach trip in 1966. Enjoying a trip to Marineland are Leslie Jordan, Dianne Hale, Susan Hale, Janet Jordan, Joan Hale and Jana Jordan. In back, Raymond Hale, Allen and Peggy Jordan.

Although Ann and I were involved in business, community and church activities, we were never too busy for a vacation at the beach with our family and friends. Every summer "fun in the sun" at Daytona Beach, Florida, was a treat for our family. The Jordan family, Allen, Peggy, Leslie, Jana and Janet, joined us for our beach vacations.

Sporting Mickey Mouse ears on a Florida trip to Disney World, the Hale and Jordan children enjoy visiting Cinderella's castle. Jana and Janet Jordan are in front of Joan, Susan and Dianne Hale in June 1972.

Our destination in July 1971 was "The Hawaiian Inn", a new luxury resort on the beach. Riding the waves, collecting shells and building sand castles entertained the children. The best treats were buying "beach dogs" (hot dogs) from the vendor on the beach at lunchtime and choosing our favorite ice cream flavors at Howard Johnson's in the evening after dinner.

Excursions to nearby attractions included Disney World, Kennedy Space Center, Silver Springs, and Marineland. The children were thrilled to visit the nearby tourist areas that were advertised.

For enjoyment around the pool, the Activity Director planned entertainment for the guests. The men were invited to participate in a "beauty-less" contest. Our girls, Susan, Joan, Dianne and Jana and Janet Jordan, encouraged me and a friend to compete for the title, "Miss Beauty-less." They had fun dressing us for the "runway" in items of women's clothing to best display our talents. To melodic Hawaiian music the contestants paraded for the crowd. When the entrants were judged, my friend won first place, and I came in

Raymond entertains poolside guests in a "Miss Beauty-less" pageant at the Hawaiian Inn, Daytona Beach, Florida in 1971.

second place. We were winners! By the way, only three men were vying for the coveted "first place" title of "Miss Beauty-less." With family and friends cheering, we had a good time entertaining the poolside guests.

Weeks at the beach always ended too soon. For the children, leaving the beach until another year was a sad departure. As we viewed the blue skies, cotton-like clouds, and gliding seagulls on a foaming ocean, Ann and I knew this was the perfect setting for a summer vacation with family and friends – Daytona Beach, Florida.

Our Daughters are off to College

By January 1979 our daughters were attending or graduated from college. Susan graduated from Auburn University with a Bachelor of Science degree in Business Administration with a major in Marketing and was employed by TVA. (Tennessee Valley Authority). Joan graduated from the University of Alabama with a Bachelor of Science degree in Commerce and Business Administration with a major in Marketing and had enrolled in the University's graduate program to pursue a Master of Arts degree in Marketing Research. Dianne entered Auburn University in the fall of 1978 dedicated to receiving a Bachelor of Science degree in Business Administration with a major in Marketing and enjoying all aspects of college life.

Our home at 7024 Pauline Circle was built in 1974 while I was developing the Ledford Acres Subdivision. We lived there from 1974-1990.

In 1990, after the children had gone to college and married, we built a home at 7022 Pauline Circle to "downsize" our living space.

To avoid "empty nest syndrome," Ann was persuaded to come to the office and learn the real estate business so she could help with the company if I were ill or injured. She was licensed January 1, 1979, as an Affiliate Broker and trained to become a Real Estate Broker in 1981. Ann came to the office, attended education sessions, participated in the Board of REAL-TORS committees and "fell in love" with the real estate business. From that time forward she has taken an active part in Hale Realty, and the subdivisions, offices and apartments we have developed.

The Ledford Apartments complex was opened in the fall of 1979.

Chapter 12
SUCCESSFUL SEVENTIES

Developing the Ledford Farmland

After building homes and offices for a decade, the opportunity came for me to buy twenty acres of land on North Concord Road from Ann's grandmother, Mrs. A. J. Ledford. The Ledford family farm had produced vegetables, flowers and dairy products to sell at

Raymond oversees the construction of the Ledford Apartments in 1979.

Blueprints of the apartments are reviewed by Ann and Raymond as the interior design is planned.

the old "Market House" which was later demolished to make way for the Patten Parkway Memorial. When the farmland was no longer cultivated, it was sold to me for development and the new subdivision of Ledford Acres was platted for thirty-eight new homes.

After experiencing the devastating floods in the Woodmore community in the spring of 1973, Ann and I moved to higher ground in the fast growing area of East Brainerd.

Two of the streets in Ledford Acres, Pauline Circle and Raymond Court, were named for my parents. At 7024 Pauline Circle Ann and I built a home where we lived for nineteen years until our daughters were graduated from college and married. In 1990 we "downsized" into a home next door where we are now living at 7022 Pauline Circle.

On five acres along the I-75 freeway, a one hundred twenty-one unit apartment complex, The Ledford Apartments, was built. Construction began in March 1979 and tenants were occupying the first group of apartments by the fall of that year. Quality construction included concrete insulated block walls with brick veneer facing, mansard roofs and electric heat pumps.

While the apartments were being built, Ann returned to the University of Tennessee at Chattanooga for an Interior Design course. She chose the colors, wallpapers, paneling and carpets to give the units a beautifully coordinated style.

Roy Kincer was painting contractor for the Ledford Apartments. In the 1960's, Roy, who became a life-long friend, began working with Raymond painting offices, apartments and new subdivision homes.

Lamar Williams was in charge of maintenance at the Ledford Apartments.

Lamar Williams, who worked with me in the construction business, became my first maintenance man. He kept the complex in excellent condition – including the pool and deck. The swimming pool at the apartments was a special pleasure for my children and grandchildren.

My four year old grandson was excited when he saw a new drink machine being delivered from the Coca-Cola Company. He ran to put his quarter in the machine for a Coke. After he received a cold drink the machine returned his quarter. Later I heard him tell his friends, "Go get a Coke. The machine is giving away free drinks." Profits from the drink machine were slim that summer.

As a treat for the tenants each summer, Ann and I sponsored a picnic and pool party. The Ledford Apartment club room was the location for many good times. Memories were made as we hosted bridal showers, celebrated birthdays, gathered for church socials and entertained with pool parties and picnics for many of our friends, as well as family. Friendships were formed that have lasted through the years.

Each summer, a picnic and pool party was hosted by Raymond and Ann for tenants at the Ledford Apartments. At this happy occasion in July 1982 are, seated, Kay Westbrook, Marie Huber, and Jo Ann Hearn, apartment manager. Standing are Eddie Zarzour, Pam Bowman, David Cornelius, Jim Fry and Joel Hollis, later my stockbroker with UBS.

Celebrating Anniversaries

Family anniversaries and birthdays are occasions to celebrate. Edith and Durand Ledford, Ann's parents, were honored on their Golden Wedding Anniversary in May of 1976 when an open house was hosted at our home on Pauline Circle. Aunts, uncles, cousins and friends arrived to make it a festive occasion.

C. Durand and Edith Ledford, Ann's parents, celebrated their Golden Wedding Anniversary in May 1976 with a reception at the home of Raymond and Ann at 7024 Pauline Circle.

In June 1977, Ann and I celebrated our Silver Wedding Anniversary. Our daughters, Susan, Joan and Dianne, honored us with a reception at our home at 7024 Pauline Circle. On a beautiful day we welcomed

Raymond and Ann celebrated their Silver Anniversary in 1977 at their home with a lovely reception hosted by their daughters. Pictured with them (from left) are Joan, Dianne and Susan.

family and friends to celebrate our twenty-five years of happy marriage.

Central Baptist Church Celebrates "Twenty Years and More"

Central Baptist Church, our home church, celebrated twenty years in the Woodmore Community in 1978. For the anniversary celebration Ann was chairman of the history committee which outlined activities for the month of June. Each Sunday was a special occasion with honored guests, receptions and a pageant of the past, "Twenty Years and More – including the Seventy-One Before," written and produced by Gail Pike.

Central Baptist Church, 1978

Central Baptist Church celebrated 20 years in the Woodmore community during the entire month of June 1978. A church history, *Twenty Years and More*, written by Dr. Elizabeth Landress Dalton, was published by Roy McDonald of the *Chattanooga News-Free Press*. Pictured at the celebration introducing the book were Raymond Hale and Mr. and Mrs. Roy McDonald.

The "crown jewel" of the celebration was the publishing and dedication of the church history book, *Twenty Years and More.* As Research Editor, Ann compiled information to be included in the book written by Dr. Elizabeth Landress Dalton. Mr. D. A. Landress, Dr. Dalton's father, was a charter member of the church which was established on January 13, 1887. He wrote the first church history in 1937, "The Golden Jubilee of Central Baptist Church." It is appropriate that his daughter, Elizabeth, continued to record the church history.

Roy McDonald, owner and publisher of the *Chattanooga News-Free Press*, provided the skills of his employees in designing and publishing the book. Pete Hunter, a Graphic Artist with the newspaper and a Central Baptist Church member, prepared the perfectly arranged layout.

"Mr. Roy" used his resources and expertise in printing the book with the newspapers' first computers. Watching the huge, newly acquired pieces of equipment translate the typed pages into a text for a permanent, printed history was a fascinating experience – and on the "cutting edge of progress." Roy McDonald and his family were honored guests the evening of the book presentation and dedication on June 25, 1978.

"Mr. Roy" Honors REALTORS

Not only was "Mr. Roy" generous with the churches in the area, but also with professional organizations including the REALTORS. Through the *Chattanooga News-Free Press* he publicized meetings, conventions and awards for REALTORS. During his ownership of the newspaper publicity for real estate companies and activities was outstanding.

In 1978, the *Chattanooga News-Free Press* hosted an open house at the newspaper honoring members of the Chattanooga Association of REALTORS. Enjoying the occasion are Paula Stone and Eloise Hixson, Secretaries at Hale Realty; Curtis Adams, Circulation Manager; Raymond Hale, Hale Realty; and Jim McNelly, Classified Advertising Editor.

In 1979 "Mr. Roy" honored members of the Chattanooga Association of REALTORS with a reception at his publishing company in appreciation for REALTORS advertising in his newspaper. Paula Stone and Eloise Hixon, my efficient secretaries for over twenty years, accompanied me to the party. Each of them played an important part in the early development of Hale Realty.

Chattanooga Board of REALTORS Builds an Office

The Chattanooga Board of REALTORS, a small group of real estate agents who were optimistic about the future growth of the real estate industry in Chattanooga, occupied a small office in the Jackson Building on Cherry Street in 1978. As the number of agents

As Building Committee Chairman, Raymond presented construction plans at the ground breaking for the new Chattanooga Board of REALTORS building on Amnicola Highway in 1978.

grew, the office staff was increased requiring additional office space. In keeping with our profession as REALTORS, we wanted to own our own real estate.

The REALTORS chose a Site Selection Committee to search for a location for a new office building convenient to all areas of Hamilton County. I acted as Building Committee Chairman to oversee the planning, bidding and construction of the new building. T. U. Parks Construction Company built the 3800 square foot building for $152,000.

At 3501 Amnicola Highway an attractive and efficiently designed office building became the new home of The Chattanooga Board of REALTORS.

Chapter 13
OUR DAUGHTERS SAY "I DO"

After graduating from the colleges of their choice and choosing careers, Susan, Joan and Dianne married. Joan was the first. While at the University of Alabama, Joan met David Wayne Bunn from Bessemer, Alabama, and they were married on July 10, 1982, at Central Baptist Church, Chattanooga, Tennessee.

The following year on June 18, 1983, Susan married Mitchell Curtis Chastain also at Central Baptist Church. Brainerd Baptist Church was Dianne's choice for her wedding to Michael Ricardo Gonzalez on February 26, 1994.

From their unions seven children were born – our seven wonderful grandchildren.

Jennifer Susan Chastain born April 11, 1984
Brandon Douglas Bunn born June 15, 1987
Brad Franklin Chastain born July 23, 1987
Tyler Durand Bunn born March 4, 1992
Davis Alexander Bunn born March 4, 1992
Cameron Michael Gonzalez born June 28, 1995
Alex Christopher Gonzalez born December 3, 1998

Linda Joan Hale married David Wayne Bunn of Bessemer, Alabama, on July 10, 1982, at Central Baptist Church in Chattanooga, Tennessee.

Susan Duranne Hale married Mitchell Curtis Chastain on June 18, 1983, at Central Baptist Church, Chattanooga, Tennessee.

Edith Dianne Hale married Michael Ricardo Gonzalez on February 26, 1994, at Brainerd Baptist Church in Chattanooga, Tennessee.

The Viar family from Halls, Tennessee, attended Joan's wedding and reception. With Ann and Raymond are Sherry and Phil Crihfield; seated, Montine Viar Robertson and Virginia Viar Austin.

Attending the weddings were Ann's high school and college friends. Pictured are Marnie Abel, Ann, Bettye Taylor, Jane Isbell, Nancy Williams, Rosemary Winn and Joan Rorex.

A daughter's wedding celebration included Dr. David and Jane Isbell, Peggy and Lee Wallace, Marnie and Jim Abel, and Dr. Larry and Susan Fogo, pictured with Ann and Raymond.

Wedding guests were Kent and Elizabeth Fortenberry with Kevin, Albert, Jr. and Alice Waller and Albert Waller, Sr.

Chapter 14
POTPOURRI

National Women's Council of REALTORS' Installation

Through the years Ann and I have developed friendships on the local, state and national levels of Realtor organizations. Our friend, Bettye Harrison, a Chattanooga REALTOR and leader in the real estate

Raymond and Ann with President Bettye and George Harrison at the National Women's Council of REALTORS' installation in New Orleans in 1985

industry, served as National Women's Council of RE-ALTORS President in 1986. She invited me to be the Installing Officer at her installation as National President in New Orleans, Louisiana, in November 1985. Ann and I attended the national convention and celebrated with Bettye and her husband George amid southern traditions of ball gowns, "king cakes," jazz, cable cars and tours of antebellum homes.

Halls Homecoming 1986

"Reflections of The '40's" was the theme of Halls Homecoming 1986. Activities in July 1986 included a historical display at the Town Hall, an air show at the old Air Force Base and the 40th reunion of Halls High School Class of '46.

Raymond is happily packing for a trip to "Halls Homecoming '86"

School Principal James "Jim" and Mary Ann Peery returned for the Halls High School 40th Reunion where Jim was guest speaker.

One of the highlights of my life was attending my fortieth class reunion. Wanting to make a good appearance, Ann and I packed our best "duds" and headed for Halls to renew acquaintances and visit with family.

Prior to the Friday night banquet, a small committee met at classmate Madeline Cherry Vaden's home to complete plans for the weekend. As I stepped onto the porch, another lady arrived at the same time and we chatted a few minutes before anyone came to the door.

I asked her "Now, what is your name?"

"Evelyn Bryan," she replied.

I was startled and embarrassed because I didn't recognize her. Evelyn was my high school "sweetheart" – but, after all, forty years had passed since seeing my high school friends.

As Master of Ceremonies for the Friday night banquet, I welcomed friends from near and far. James

"Jim" Peery and his wife Mary Ann came from Apopka, Florida, to Chattanooga and traveled with us to the reunion. Jim was a favorite uncle who became coach and principal of Halls High School in the Fall of 1946 after returning from World War II. He and his family moved to Apopka, Florida, in the late 1950's where Jim held the position of high school principal until his retirement. As guest speaker at the reunion he delighted classmates with stories of the "good ole days" at Halls High.

Cousins Billy and Bobby Steelman, school buddies from my early years, attended the reunion. Billy was an Air Force officer at the Pentagon and Bobby had taken over the family farming business. Both were successful in their chosen careers.

Wymond Hurt, one of my best friends through the years, returned from Tupelo, Mississippi, for the celebration. Ann and I attended Halls First Baptist

Attending Halls First Baptist Church at "Homecoming '86" were Wymond Hurt, Sr., Linda Hurt, Raymond and Ann Hale, and Wymond Hurt, Jr.

Church, our home church in the 1950's, with Wymond, his wife Linda and Dad, Wymond Hurt, Sr. Mr. Hurt, Sr. employed me at his Western Auto Store and was a wonderful mentor in my high school years. Wymond and I have kept in touch through the years as our lives have evolved from boyhood chums to senior citizens.

The Army Air Base, a central part of Halls' economic and social life in the 1940's, closed following World War II. For the homecoming celebration a variety of vintage planes were flown to the base for a display and air show. Seeing airplanes on the base again was a reminder of the intense training of pilots and the importance of the Army Air Base in the war effort.

Raymond returned to Halls, Tennessee, in 1986 to celebrate the 40th anniversary of his graduation from Halls High School. Raymond was Master of Ceremonies for the reunion program and is pictured standing third from left with classmates.

Halls Homecoming '86 and a fortieth class re-union are emblazoned in my memory bank of special occasions. What a wonderful way to reconnect with family and friends and step back in time to the "fabulous 40's."

Pat Rose Elected Commissioner

Pat Rose, a Christian gentleman of honesty and integrity, led Chattanooga as Mayor from 1975 to 1983, a time of unprecedented change and progress in our city. Under his guidance, Chattanooga began

TO LEAD ROSE'S CAMPAIGN — Pat Rose announced the appointment of Raymond Hale as manager of his campaign for the office of commissioner of the Public Utilities Department in the upcoming city election. Pictured from left are Mr. Hale and his wife, Ann; at right, Mr. Rose and his wife, Carolyn. (Staff photo by Steve Grider)

Rose Selects Executive Raymond Hale As Campaign Head For Utilities Run

its rebirth as a business, financial and tourist center of the South. After declining to run for a third term as Mayor, Rose entered the world of private enterprise for several years.

With the 1987 city election approaching, Pat was encouraged to run for the City Council position of Commissioner of Public Works. To lead a large group of supporters he selected me as campaign manager. We worked vigorously and enthusiastically and brought an overwhelming victory to Rose in April 1987. He returned to public service as Commissioner of Public Works on the Chattanooga City Council where he remained until his retirement in 1991.

Chattanooga Association of REALTORS Celebrates Its "Diamond Jubilee"

The Chattanooga Association of REALTORS commemorated seventy five years of service to Realtors and the Chattanooga community with a "Diamond Jubilee" celebration in 1987. A year long celebration was planned and implemented by Ann with the assistance of her "Jubilee" committee.

William A. Moore, a Denver, Colorado REALTOR and President of the National Association of REALTORS, honored Chattanooga REALTORS by bringing greetings to the local group. He predicted "there will be growth in housing sales through 1987 since fixed rate

During the "Diamond Jubilee" celebrating the 75th anniversary of the Chattanooga Association of REALTORS, the past presidents were honored with a dinner at the Walden Club. Eddie Nicholson, "The Rocking Chair Philosopher," delighted the guests with his good natured humor and stories. Pictured are June Kempson, executive officer of the Association, Eddie Nicholson, guest speaker, Raymond Hale and Ann Hale, Chairman of the celebration.

home mortgage rates are down to 9.62 percent – about half the 17.5 percentage peak five years ago."

As part of the celebration, past presidents of the Chattanooga Association of REALTORS were recognized at a dinner at the Walden Club. Eddy Nicholson, "The Rocking Chair Philosopher," delighted guests with his tall tales and down-home humor.

The highlight of the "Diamond Jubilee" was Miss America, Kellye Cash, a native Tennessean, performing

Miss America, Kellye Cash, is with Ann and Raymond at the "Diamond Jubilee."

a musical program at the Imperial Ballroom of the Chattanooga Choo-Choo. David Carroll of Channel 3 served as Master of Ceremonies as a large crowd gathered to celebrate seventy-five years of history of the Chattanooga Association of REALTORS.

Returning To Hawaii

In 1987 the National Association of REALTORS returned to Honolulu, Hawaii, for the annual convention. Ann and I arrived in the islands safely, but our four pieces of luggage were nowhere to be found. For convenience on the first night the hotel management gave us an emergency kit with a few items and two dinner tickets.

Raymond and Ann dining at the 1987 National Association of REALTORS convention in Hawaii.

The second day – no luggage, even though I called the airport every few hours to check the results of the search. When Ann exclaimed, "I don't have a thing to wear!" – it was the truth. Ann began to shop and what fun she had!

The third day the hotel manager called to tell us two of the four pieces of luggage had arrived at the hotel. Rushing to claim the bags, I discovered the only luggage found was mine. Ann's two pieces of new luggage were never located. Sooo – off to the malls for another shopping spree!

"Dancing With The Stars" – 1987 version – was a highlight of the entertainment at the installation banquet on the final evening of the convention. To the delight of the Realtors a lively band played 1950's music. Ann and I were seated with friends at a dinner table near the stage when the band leader called me to the stage for "audience participation." To the cheers of my friends and without missing a beat, I danced a "jitterbug" number with the performers. No trophy was presented for my lively performance but I had more fun than anyone.

"Dancing with the Stars" – 1987 version – included Raymond who was invited to join the entertainers on stage to dance to a lively tune.

Chapter 15
MOVING TO EAST BRAINERD

A New Location for Hale Realty

In 1987 the Ledford Apartments had a ninety-five percent occupancy rate and a competent office manager, Louise Bunn, our daughter's mother-in-law. Time had come to focus on and relocate Hale Realty.

East Brainerd was an expanding community with growth sparked by the developing and opening of

The new Hale Realty building at 7540 East Brainerd Road was completed in January 1988.

Attending Hale Realty open house in the new huilding is Vernon Cox, Chairman of the Board, President CEO of Inter Fed Savings and Loan Company, pictured with Raymond.

Hamilton Place Mall. East Brainerd Road was a two-lane road with a wide selection of residential properties destined for commercial development. After careful consideration Ann and I chose a two and one-half acre tract at 7540 East Brainerd Road to purchase. The home on the property was rented for several years before it was removed. We developed plans for a new office building and construction began in the summer of 1987.

A contemporary style building for Hale Realty opened in January 1988 amidst a deluge of snow. Susan Hale Chastain, our oldest daughter, joined the company as office and marketing manager. Ann and I embarked on the enterprising experience of building an outstanding real estate company, Hale Realty, in the fastest growing community in Hamilton County. Within a few years East Brainerd Road was expanded to five lanes and businesses "sprung up" along this rapidly growing corridor.

Our youngest daughter, Dianne, completed our "family management team" in January 1989 when

Dianne Hale Gonzalez is shown with her first child, Cameron, 8 months old.

she joined Hale Realty as secretary. She and Susan provided secretarial assistance, training and encourage-

ment for the staff and real estate agents during the early 1990's as the company grew. Dianne worked with Hale Realty until February 1995 when she resigned to be home and await the birth in June of her first son, Cameron.

After Dianne's departure to raise a family, Sandi Word Case came to work for Hale

Sandi Case with husband, Mike, and daughters, Rebecca and Cassie

Realty as a secretary in June 1995. Sandi graduated from Northwest Junior College with a degree in Business Administration. She brought computer skills and technology expertise to our staff. Sandi kept us on the "cutting edge of progress." In 2009 Sandi, a loyal secretary and friend, continues to work for Hale Realty. She has assisted us by entering the text of this book into the computer for editing.

Hale Realty agents donated time and energy to community charities. A favorite project was wrapping gifts at Hamilton Place Mall for "Kids On The Block." Our agents joined in the Christmas spirit for several years by greeting shoppers and wrapping packages for the "Kids."

At Christmastime, Hale Realty wrapped packages for "Kids On The Block" at Hamilton Place Mall. Pictured are Sally Wagner, Elaine Peterson, Ronnie Hogan, Vicki Trapp, W. A. "Dub" Thompson, Madeleine Johnson, Eva Jo Smith, Cathy Hendren, and back row, Ann Hale, Sandy Wright, and Virginia Brandon.

A popular organization in the Chattanooga area is Bethel Bible Village, a home for children ages 4-17 whose families are in crisis and cannot care for them. The mission of the Village is to provide safe, nurturing and Christ-centered homes for children and to inspire them to live productive Christian lives. Each year Hale Realty participated in

Pat Boone sponsors the Bethel Bible School Celebrity Golf Tournament each year. Hale Realty participated in 1991.

the annual Village Golf Tournament, a popular event sponsored by Pat Boone.

In addition to Kids On The Block and Bethel Bible Village Golf Tournament, Hale agents were generous in their support of community charities including The United Way, Salvation Army, Heart Fund, and Clifton Hills Elementary School.

Ann Receives Honors

In 1989 Ann was honored as "Tennessee Member of The Year" by the state chapter of Women's Council

To highlight and honor people who helped make its history, the Chattanooga Board of REALTORS created a "Wall of Presidents." Ann Hale, center, Chairman of the History Committee, led the group in researching the pictures and biographies of the past presidents of the Board. Surrounding her are June Kempson, executive vice-president of the Chattanooga Board of REALTORS, Joyce Siniard, John R. McGauley, Janet Fisher, Floss Anderson, Carl Clift, Jr., and Mary Ruth Cook

Designated Tennessee Member of the Year by Women's Council of REALTORS, Ann received recognition at the state convention (TAR) in 1989.

of REALTORS. She served as Tennessee Chapter WCR president in 1987. She previously held the office of Chattanooga Chapter President in 1983 and the following year was designated by the local WCR chapter as 1984 "Woman of The Year." In 1996 Ann served as Tennessee Governor for the National Women's Council of REALTORS. Many hours of involvement in and commitment to the Women's Council of REALTORS preceded these recognitions.

As Chairman of the Chattanooga Association of REALTORS' History Committee, Ann led the group to research and designed a picture "Wall of Presidents" to highlight and recognize presidents who influenced Association history. Members and guests enjoy visiting the presidential display and reflecting on the leadership and accomplishments of the Association through the years.

A quote lingers in our minds: "You can't know where you are going until you understand where you have been." The Chattanooga Association of REALTORS, since its establishment in 1912, has a rich history of enhancing the real estate profession and protecting private property rights.

After years of dedicated service to the real estate industry through the Chattanooga Association of REALTORS, Ann was honored as 1991 "REALTOR of The Year". In 2007 the Association moved into a new multi-million dollar building at 2963 Amnicola Highway. The tradition of excellence continues in the twenty-first century.

After being designated Chattanooga Association of REALTORS 1991 "REALTOR of the Year," Ann is joined by her husband Raymond and daughters Susan and Dianne.

Real Estate Company Merger

January 1, 1990, Elgin Smith, a REALTOR and good friend since 1958, merged Elgin Smith Realtors, Inc., with Hale Realty which became one of the largest, most progressive agencies in Chattanooga. Our agents blended their skills, talents and personalities into a flourishing "business" family. We shared good times with agents at summer picnics, award banquets and Christmas parties in our home. Elgin and I worked together in a successful, productive real estate business for over thirteen years.

Ann's and my friendship with Elgin and Jean Smith has extended through the years as we traveled to real

1996 Hale Realty Awards. Seated: Susan French, Donna Schmitt, Bruce Gilpatrick, Vicki Trapp, Jim Downey, Sherre Bales, Wilda Lewis, Gina Mason. Standing: Susan Chastain, Sandi Case, JoAnn Greene, Julie Chamberlain, Dub Thompson, Gayla Choate, Raymond Hale, Ann Hale, Elgin Smith, JoAnn Sims, Heman McDade, Nanelle Jeffries, Margie Longacre, Pam Jackson.

Hale, Elgin Smith Firms Merge

Elgin Smith Realtors, Inc. has announced plans to merge with Hale Realty, effective January 1, 1990. Shown at the Hale Realty offices in East Brainerd are, seated from left, Mrs. Elgin (Jean) Smith and Susan Jensen. Standing, from left, are Elgin Smith, Ann Hale and Raymond Hale. With the merger, Hale Realty became the largest real estate firm in East Brainerd.

estate meetings, shared dinner parties and attended church activities at Brainerd Baptist Church where we continue to share our faith and friendship.

Pilgrimage To The Holy Land

In July 1993, Ann and I went on the "trip of a life-time" – a pilgrimage to the Holy Land. The Reverend Ansell T. Baker, our Pastor at Central Baptist Church

Pictured by the Sea of Galilee in July 1993, Raymond and Ann (right) and friends Don and Martha Erwin (left) joined The Reverend Ansell T. Baker and wife Sue on a tour of Israel.

in Woodmore for twenty years, with his wife Sue, led the tour of over forty travelers to Israel. As we rode and walked where Jesus and his disciples walked, Brother Baker quoted from memory the appropriate scriptures to enhance this wonderful experience.

The most memorable tour in the Holy Land was to Masada, Israel, the boat-shaped mountain in the desert. On the eastern slopes of the Jordan Desert, Masada rises 1,440 feet above the shore of the Dead Sea. A cable car took our tour group from the desert sands to the summit of Masada. The surface area of 2,130 feet by 984 feet provided space to sustain a community of people atop the mountain.

In the first century King Herod the Great, fleeing from Roman rule, built two elaborate palaces on Masada. The "hanging palace" on the northern end of the summit extended 115 feet down the mountain on three levels connected by winding staircases.

The larger palace was located on the western side of the mountain. During Herod's occupation a wall was erected around the perimeter of Masada and watch towers were positioned along the wall. In addition, one lookout station was placed in the center of the summit from which all areas could be monitored.

Two routes provided access to Masada. On the east side the "snakepath" ascended over 1,000 feet from the desert floor. The 328 foot Roman ramp on the western side was built by Jewish forced labor during the Roman siege of 70-73 A.D.

At the beginning of the Great Revolt against Rome, Jewish zealots captured Masada from the Roman garrison stationed there. The group of refugees built a synagogue, public hall and ritual baths. Others joined them until the community totaled approximately 1,000. The Roman armies arrived in 72 A.D. and the seizure of the mountain lasted several months. When there was no hope of escape the Jews in Masada chose to die rather than live as slaves under Rome. The

A lookout station was located in the center of Masada to monitor all areas of the summit.

destruction of the fortress and mass suicide by the Jews occurred on the night before the Roman Tenth Legion took Masada.

Since 1965 Masada has been a tourist attraction. Ancient history came alive as we walked where the Jewish people lived, fought and died, dedicated to their freedom which did not come for another 1,000 years. The descent from the summit of the mountain offers picturesque, breath-taking views of blue skies, desert sands and the Dead Sea. An unforgettable trip to Masada is a must if you go to Israel.

Our friends, Martha and Don Erwin, were on the tour with us. One of the most inspirational moments of the trip was at the site of the crucifixion and burial of Jesus. The tour group gathered at a site overlooking the Garden Tomb to pray and take communion. From this location, we could see Golgotha—the place believed to be the site of the crucifixion of Jesus. Don led us in several songs, including "The Old Rugged Cross," and Brother Baker prayed for the tour group and our safe return home.

Ledford Apartments Damaged By Tornado

As Ann and I watched the Lady Vols play for the basketball championship on Good Friday, March 28, 1997, we noticed tornado warnings scrolling across the television screen. Since tornados are not

The Ledford Apartments received damages in excess of $225,000 in the March 1997 tornado.

characteristic of this area, we ignored the warnings and went to bed.

After 1 A.M. I received a call from Louise Bunn, the apartment manager, telling me, "You better come down to the apartments. Some of the people do not have electricity."

I sleepily responded, "Well, if you don't mind, let's wait until morning. I can't do anything about it tonight."

After hanging up the phone, checking out the problem seemed the appropriate thing to do. When I arrived at the apartments, half of the units were damaged by the tornado that moved through East Brainerd early Saturday morning. The heavy dumpster was blown across the parking lot. Windows were broken and cars damaged. The neighborhood looked like a war zone with trees and debris blocking roads. Homes were damaged and many people displaced.

The skies were crystal clear with only a few white clouds as Saturday morning dawned. To get the apartments back in "living condition" as quickly as possible, painters, roofers, heat and air conditioning technicians, and glass replacement companies were called. With so much damage in the area supplies and workers would be in great demand. Calling early and being first on their lists was important.

The glass company brought four trucks and all the glass they had in stock and began working immediately on Saturday morning to replace three hundred windows. By the afternoon, 6,000 squares of roofing were delivered to the premises for roofers to begin work on Monday morning.

The Red Cross canteen truck arrived on the scene to distribute sandwiches and drinks to the distraught tenants and tired and dedicated workers. The tenants were understanding and cooperative. The apartment units were repaired within a week after the tornado and the renters could return to their own apartments.

There were many repairs and replacements to the complex still to be completed. The weather was beautiful with no rain for the next six weeks and work was "humming" along at a rapid pace. As the repairs neared completion, I wanted to reward the laborers who had worked so diligently. On a Friday afternoon, they were called together outside my office at 4 P.M. I thanked them for their loyalty and dedication to me and the task of repairing the apartments. As a surprise

Raymond rewards workmen with $20 bills. Pictured are Louise Bunn, apartment manager, Tommy Perdue, maintenance superintendent, and Raymond.

for the forty-five workers each was given a $20 bill. "I want you fellows to be here on Monday because the repairs need to be completed as soon as possible."

On Monday by 10 o'clock in the morning only a few laborers arrived to work. I asked the superintendent, "What happened to the men?"

He replied, "You shouldn't have given them the $20 bills. They probably got drunk and have a "hangover." The thought of the workers spending their money in the wrong places and not coming to work on Monday didn't occur to me when I rewarded them with extra dollars.

After six months of extensive repairs, The Ledford Apartments were in excellent condition. Ann and I had owned the apartments for almost twenty years. It was time to say "good bye" to the most successful and rewarding real estate development of my career. In September of 1998 ownership of The Ledford Apartments was transferred to a new investor.

The sparkling clear water in the swimming pool at the Ledford Apartments was inviting to tenants, guests, friends and family.

Chapter 16
ENTERING THE TWENTY-FIRST CENTURY

Millennial Year of 2000

The excitement of entering the millennial year of 2000 was electric. REALTORS anticipated a decade of progress and expansion of opportunities in housing and development in the Chattanooga and North Georgia areas.

In the year 2000 Ann served as President of the Chattanooga Association of REALTORS. Traveling to represent the Association, meeting with committees and writing articles for trade publications occupied much of her time. When Ann was installed as CAR president, we became the only husband and wife to each have the honor of the presidency and to receive "REALTOR of the Year" awards.

Changes were coming rapidly in the real estate industry as sophisticated computer technology, electronic key boxes and Regional Multiple Listing Systems were changing and improving the way we did business. The most significant emphasis was on state and

Ann Hale was installed as 2000 Chattanooga Association of RE-ALTORS president at the annual Christmas party at the Chattanooga Golf and Country Club. She is flanked by daughter, Susan Chastain, Hale Realty office manager, and husband, Raymond.

Attending Ann's installation were daughters and sons-in-law David and Joan Bunn, Susan Chastain and Dianne and Mike Gonzalez.

Attending the REALTORS' Legislative Conference in Washington, D.C. are Contact Team members Ann Hale, Elwynn Schwartz, Randy Durham, Y. L. Coker, George Kangles and Francie Ryder, Association Executive of the Chattanooga Association of REALTORS.

national legislative issues. As members of the Tennessee Congressional Contact Team, Ann and I attended the REALTORS Legislative Conference in Washington, D.C. on many occasions through the years.

The Contact Team lobbies on proposed laws related to home ownership and private property rights. Realtors participate in one of the largest and most powerful Political Action Committees (PAC's) in the nation, donating over seven million dollars in 2007 to political candidates of the Republican and Democratic parties.

The National Association of REALTORS honored members who have served more than 40 years in the real estate industry. The award, a diamond and ruby pin, designating the member as *REALTOR emeritus*, was presented by the Chattanooga Association of REALTORS to each deserving member. The luncheon honor program was at the Chattanooga Choo-Choo on September 7, 2005, with these honorees attending. Pictured, seated, are Bill Clift, Fletcher Bright, Jim Glascock, Raymond Hale, Hugh Huffaker. Standing are Ed Fisher, Rudy Walldorf, Elgin Smith, Hugh Siniard, and Dan Griess, Chattanooga Association of REALTORS president.

PAC funds collected by Realtor Associations do not buy votes, but the donations are distributed among candidates who support private property rights and issues that positively affect the real estate industry.

Designation as REALTOR Emeritus

REALTOR Emeritus is the designation given by the National Association of REALTORS to members who serve the real estate industry more than forty years. The award, a diamond and ruby lapel pin, was presented to deserving REALTORS at an awards luncheon at the Chattanooga Choo-Choo on September 7, 2005.

At that time my contributions as a REALTOR extended over forty nine years in sales management, building and developing. My comment to the audience was, "Reflecting on my years in real estate, I enjoyed the business. It has been good to me and my family."

Traveling Buddies through the Years

Since our "Woodmore Days" Ann and I have enjoyed many good times with special friends, Bettye and Worth (Poss) Powell. Atlanta and Pigeon Forge are our favorite travel destinations. Shopping is great in both places and at Christmastime twinkling lights illuminate the streets and shopping centers. Choosing a favorite restaurant at the end of the day is always a delight.

Our special friends, Worth "Poss" and Bettye Powell, are travel "buddies" who have joined us for short trips to the Smokie Mountains and Atlanta for over 30 years. Raymond and Ann are pictured with their friends in Pigeon Forge at the Dixie Stampede in May, 2007.

At this time only a few streets separate our homes in the East Brainerd area. We cherish the friendship and wonderful memories of good times shared through the years.

Celebrating Our Golden Wedding Anniversary

On June 22, 2002, Ann and I celebrated our Golden Wedding Anniversary when Susan Chastain, Joan and David Bunn, and Dianne and Mike Gonzalez hosted a dinner party in our honor at the Walden Club in Chattanooga, Tennessee. Golden balloons, family pictures, and monogrammed candy bars added to the festivities. Guests were served a fillet mignon dinner cooked to order and delicious "wedding cake."

Brother Ansell T. Baker and his wife Sue joined us from Athens, Tennessee. Our wedding was his first as Pastor of Central Baptist Church in the early 1950's. Joan Speakman Rorex, Ann's friend since first grade and maid-of-honor at our wedding, came from Little Rock, Arkansas, for the occasion. Ann and I were thrilled that other members of the wedding party also returned to celebrate our fifty years of marriage.

Raymond and Ann Hale cut the cake while celebrating their 50th wedding anniversary at the Walden Club on June 22, 2002.

My how the years fly by! It seems only "yesterday" we said our wedding vows on a hot, sultry Sunday afternoon and embarked on life's adventures – a very successful, rewarding and happy journey.

Friends attending the Golden Anniversary celebration are, left to right, The Reverend Ansell T. and Sue Baker; Don and Martha Erwin; Raymond and Ann, the honorees; Rudy and Dot Simpson; and Hugh and Joy Siniard.

The Hale family at the 50th Wedding Anniversary Celebration. Front row: Alex and Cameron Gonzalez, Ann Hale, Tyler and Davis Bunn; Back row: Susan Chastain, Brad and Jennifer Chastain, Brandon Bunn, Joan Bunn, Raymond Hale, David Bunn, Dianne and Mike Gonzalez.

Ann's high school and college friends, who attended the wedding in 1952, helped celebrate the Golden Anniversary at the Walden Club. Pictured are Bill and Bettye Taylor; Dr. Larry and Susan Fogo; Joan Rorex; Raymond and Ann, the honorees; Jim and Marnie Abel; Bob and Nancy Williams; and Dr. David and Jane Isbell.

Chapter 17
LET ME TELL YOU ABOUT MY GRANDCHILDREN

THE CHASTAIN FAMILY
Jennifer Chastain

Jennifer, our bright and beautiful twenty-four year old granddaughter, attends graduate school at the University of Tennessee in Knoxville, Tennessee. She is the oldest grandchild and the only girl among six boys ranging in age from ten to twenty-one years.

At fourteen years of age Jennifer participated in a Mission trip to Charleston, South Carolina with World Changers, a Southern Baptist organization assisting people and churches requesting help with home and church repairs. Ironically, her group was assigned to Dorchester-Wayland Baptist Church, the church where Ann and I were members while living in Charleston.

Jennifer's middle and high school years were completed at Girls Preparatory School (GPS) where she excelled academically. Awards she received included the Latin I (8th grade), Latin III award (10th grade) and The Twentieth Century History Award in her senior year.

After graduating from GPS she worked two jobs while attending the University of Tennessee at Chattanooga pursuing a Bachelor of Science degree with majors in Mathematics and Finance. She graduated *summa cum laude* and led her class of over five hundred graduates in the processional to receive their diplomas at the McKenzie Arena in December 2006.

Jennifer will graduate in May 2009 from the University of Tennessee in Knoxville with a Master of Science degree in Statistics and pursue a career in the financial world.

Jennifer is honored as "Miss Bess T. Shepherd" in June 1995. She is pictured with her mother, Susan, after receiving her trophy.

Jennifer Susan Chastain, daughter of Susan Hale Chastain and Mitchell Curtis Chastain, is the oldest grandchild. She graduated *summa cum laude* from the University of Tennessee at Chattanooga in December 2006 with a Bachelor of Science degree in Finance. Wearing the white graduation tassel, she led her class of over 500 across the stage to receive their diplomas.

Brad Franklin Chastain, son of Susan Hale Chastain and Mitchell Curtis Chastain, attends the University of Tennessee at Knoxville and works at FedEx Corporation.

Brad Chastain

Brad, who is three years younger than Jennifer, is attending the University of Tennessee in Knoxville, Tennessee, studying for a Bachelor of Science degree with a major in Finance. *Lamba Chi Alpha*, where many of his McCallie School friends were members, was his fraternity choice.

In elementary school Brad enjoyed a variety of sports including basketball and received "The Coaches Award" for his good character and sportsmanlike conduct. His interest in sports continued while attending McCallie School and Brad played football, baseball and golf. After being hurt while playing football, he chose a different sport – baseball. His left field catch of a fly ball with the bases loaded gave McCallie an important team win over Baylor – their most famous rival.

Golf captured his interest in his high school years and he was a member of the golf team in his junior and senior years.

During Brad's high school years he earned extra spending money by helping me at Hale Realty on Saturdays and during summer vacations. We worked painting signs, cleaning offices and changing fluorescent bulbs in the office fixtures. Brad was always willing to do whatever tasks were asked of him.

His work experience also included representing the Cutco Knife Company as a salesman following his freshman year in college and learning construction skills on a home building crew.

Brad graduated from McCallie School in May 2005 and is continuing his education while working part-time at the FedEx Corporation.

In his Indian headdress, Brad observed Thanksgiving with his first grade teacher, Sylvia Kubic.

THE BUNN FAMILY
Brandon Bunn

In the Bunn family there is a tradition of excellence in the sport of golf. Having a membership at the Fox Den Country Club, the Bunn boys, Brandon, Tyler and Davis, from an early age have played golf and developed their skills with the goal of perfection.

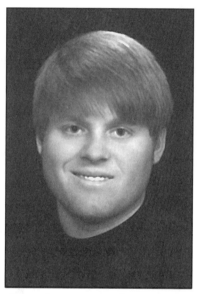

Brandon Douglas Bunn is son of Joan and David Bunn.

Brandon, who celebrated his twenty-first birthday in June 2008, is a junior on a golf scholarship at the University of Memphis in Memphis, Tennessee. In his first appearance in a college tournament Brandon posted the Tigers' lowest score in the Memphis Intercollegiate Tournament and led his team to a "top ten" finish.

Brandon played on the middle and high school golf teams at Farragut in Knoxville, Tennessee. In his freshman year he was honored as "Top Newcomer of the Year" on his team. The following year he received the "Most Valuable Player" award. After lettering in golf in his four high school years, Brandon was ranked fifth in Tennessee by Junior Golf Scoreboard at the end of his senior year.

Brandon played on the Southeastern Junior Golf Tour (SJGT) and was a winner at the Fort Payne Classic in Fort Payne, Alabama, in 2004 and 2005. With an even par stroke average he was named District Player of the Year in 2005. Brandon's "most fun win" was playing with his dad in the Men's Club Championship at the Fox Den Country Club. After thirty six golfers competed only two remained – Brandon and his dad. Brandon was the winner!

At the University of Memphis the golf team earned the privilege of playing in the 2008 NCAA Regional Tournament at the Council Fire Golf Course in Chattanooga, Tennessee. Brandon's exceptional skills and commitment in the game of golf continue to spark his team to excellence.

At three years of age Brandon swings a golf club – a glimpse into the future.

Tyler Bunn

Tyler, a junior at Farragut High School in Knoxville, Tennessee, has been interested in the sport of golf, a family tradition, since he was eight years old. With a set of clubs to match his size and age he began to practice with a commitment to master the game of golf.

In the years that followed he practiced with middle and high school teams although he could not play competi

Tyler Durand Bunn is son of Joan and David Bunn.

tive golf with the Farragut school teams because cerebral palsy limits his mobility.

At the age of fifteen Tyler was ambitious to have a job and save money for a car. He was hired by the Fox Den Country Club, where his family has a membership, to assist with many tasks including preparing for tournaments. On a hot August day in 2007, Tyler and his golfing friends were playing their usual game of golf when Tyler landed a "hole-in-one." The following article appeared in the *Knoxville News Sentinel*.

One-handed Ace for Bunn

Farragut High School sophomore Tyler Bunn left Fox Den Country Club cold and wet August 25. That's what happens when your buddies dump a cooler of ice water over you the day you make your first one-handed hole-in-one.

Yep, a one-handed hole-in-one.

Bunn, has cerebral palsy, and balancing himself on his left-arm brace he swung his Ping 5-iron with his right hand and from 113 yards out aced the par-3 13th – a difficult hole with the green flanked by water to its right.

"It was shocking" said the 15-year-old, whose twin brother Davis is a sophomore on the golf team. "Once I saw it drop in, we all went crazy."

Bunn, playing with a handful of members from the Farragut golf team, shot 3-over-par 75. He plays from the red tees at Fox Den, where his lowest score is 71.

In a golfing family like the Bunns, 71s can go unnoticed. David, the father, was a club champion at Fox Den. Tyler's older brother, Brandon, is a standout at the University of Memphis.

But Tyler's ace is the family's first, and that placed him alone in the spotlight.

"That gave him a 1-up," said Farragut golf coach Mike Driver.

Seeing his brothers and father wrapped up in the ancient game, Tyler began playing golf at age 8 and started getting "really serious" about it in the sixth grade. But he never let his physical handicap prevent him from improving his golf one.

"It was tough (at first)," said Tyler of starting the game. "But I just kept practicing at it and just kept coming out to the driving range."

While Driver said Tyler's not an official member of the golf team, he added that he might as well be considered such; he's always out practicing alongside the players. He was out playing with five members of the team Wednesday afternoon.

"He's a good player (too)," said Driver. "He hits his driver a good ways. He hits it 225 yards or 230 every time. His putts are better than mine."

"But he's a good individual more than anything. He just works on his game continuously. I see him at Fox Den hitting balls and putting all the time."

And Driver said he hopes that inspires his players.

Said Driver: "I hope the other guys say, 'He's out here working as hard as he can. Maybe I need to work harder as well.'"

Tyler, fourth from left, and Davis, far right, are pictured with the Farragut High School golf team after Tyler's hole-in-one.

Davis (on left) and Tyler (center) are juniors at Farragut High School in Knoxville, Tennessee. Brandon is a junior at University of Memphis.

Davis Bunn

Davis, a junior at Farragut High School in Knoxville, Tennessee, is a member of the 2008 Class 2-AAA Boys' State Championship golf team. Winning the state tournament was the "crown-jewel" win following a Region 2-AAA tournament championship the previous week.

Davis took to the golf course at the young age of eight years with dedication

Davis Alexander Bunn is son of Joan and David Bunn.

and determination to excel at the game of golf.

Through his middle school years he was a member of the golf team and played on the Southeastern Junior Golf Tour (SJGT) winning second and third place in the Willow Creek Junior Classic in consecutive years.

In the summer of 2008 the United States Golf Association (USGA) hosted a sectional qualifying tournament for the United States Junior Amateur at Old Fort Golf Course in Murfreesboro, Tennessee, where the best high school players participated. Davis was one of the top three players in Tennessee to qualify for the U. S. Junior Amateur which was played at the Shoal Creek Golf Club in Birmingham, Alabama. The field of players included the top 156 junior golfers in the country and Davis missed the cut for match play by only one stroke finishing 78th in the tournament. He is currently ranked 2nd in Tennessee and 21st in the country for the graduating Class of 2010 by Junior Golf Scoreboard. In the state he ranks 5th among all golfers. Davis continues to focus on his golf game to perfect his skills.

In his junior year Davis is visiting colleges and universities to preview the golf programs prior to choosing a school and accepting a scholarship. The excellence at golf continues in the Bunn family.

Twins Tyler and Davis Bunn are happily playing together on a visit to their Grandparents' home in spring 1993.

THE GONZALEZ FAMILY
Cameron Gonzalez

Cameron, an eighth grade student at Silverdale Baptist Academy, has many interests and achievements including academics, theater, music and literary composition.

Since being eligible at ten years of age, Cameron has been honored each year by the Duke University Talent Identification Program, a national education monitoring program for academic achievers. A three-year member of the Beta Club, Cameron attended the Tennessee Junior Beta Club convention in Nashville as a candidate for state vice-president in 2007.

A Star Roll student through elementary and middle schools, Cameron received an outstanding score on the national ACT test and was honored at a Tennessee recognition ceremony in Nashville. For two years he has served as Student Council President representing middle school students.

Creative writing has challenged Cameron's imagination and creativity. His literary compositions received awards and were published in Young Southern Writers and Anthology of Poetry by Young Americans.

At a young age, drama and theatrical productions captured Cameron's interest. Summer theater camps at the Chattanooga Theatre Centre prepared him for parts in several award-winning youth productions. Bayside Baptist Church also develops the talents of young people through music and drama. Cameron has performed in Christmas pageants, youth musicals and the drama "It's A Wonderful Life."

Mission service through the church gives the youth opportunity to travel to distant places to assist people and churches in need. With World Changers, a Southern Baptist youth organization for mission outreach, Cameron traveled to Springfield, Illinois, for a week of mission work in the summer of 2008. Another mission opportunity for Cameron was a student choir missions trip to Schroon Lake, New York, sponsored by Word of Life Fellowship. The student choir of his church toured and provided a Christian witness through mini-concerts, drama and street evangelism.

The People to People Ambassador Program, established by Dwight Eisenhower in 1956, has invited Cameron to the 2009 People to People World Leadership Forum in Washington, D.C. next summer. With energy and enthusiasm Cameron continues to participate and to excel in opportunities available to him.

Cameron Michael Gonzalez, son of Dianne and Michael Gonzalez, is President of the Siverdale Baptist Academy Middle School Student Council and a member of the Beta Club.

Alex Christopher Gonzalez, son of Dianne and Michael Gonzalez, and a talented athlete, excels in baseball and was on the Snowhill Recreation League's 9-year-old All-Star team in 2008.

Alex Gonzalez

Alex, our youngest grandson, is ten years old and a fourth grader at Silverdale Baptist Academy. A consistent member of the Honor roll, he is a Young Scholars Program nominee, a designation sponsored by Wake Forest University in Winston-Salem, North Carolina. To develop literary skills children are encouraged by the English Department of the University of Tennessee at Chattanooga to submit short stories and poems for publication. Alex's literary effort was rewarded when his original story was published in Young Southern Writers and he was honored at a recognition program at the Soldiers and Sailors Memorial Auditorium.

Bayside Baptist Church offers children Bible study, music, drama and sports. Awana, a Bible study and scripture memorization program for children, is sponsored by the church. Alex's dedication to the goals of Awana and to completion of the required work was rewarded when he received the "Clubber of the Year" award.

Drama and music also capture Alex's interest. As a member of the children's choir, he has participated in several musical dramas of the church, including, "It's A Wonderful Life." Ripple Productions, a Christian theatrical group, includes Alex and his brother, Cameron, on its roster of actors. Alex has performed in the musical production "Two From Galilee," and the drama "Angelos Distasay."

A talented athlete, Alex enjoys soccer, basketball, and football through the Bayside Baptist "Upward Sports" program. He excels in his favorite sport, baseball, and was a member of the 9-year old All-Star team sponsored by the Snowhill Recreation League in the summer of 2008.

With an outgoing personality and charming sense of humor, Alex is the sparkle on our family tree.

Alex and Cameron Gonzalez entertained with a song and dance performance at a Sunday School party on the lake in June 2001.

Chapter 18
EIGHTIETH BIRTHDAY CELEBRATION

Our daughters and sons-in-law gave me a wonderful eightieth birthday party at the Chattanooga Golf and Country Club on a Sunday afternoon in January. I enjoyed the time with my family. The girls had a professional photographer record the happy occasion.

Raymond and Ann, 80th birthday party

The Bunn Family: Joan, David, Tyler and Davis.
Not pictured: Brandon Bunn

The Chastain
Family: Brad,
Susan   and
Jennifer

The Gonzalez Family: Cameron, Dianne, Mike and Alex.

Bob and Jean Beck, parents of Michael Gonzalez

Raymond Franklin Hale, Jr. at age eighty.

Chapter 19
LIFE IS GOOD

On life's journey the years pass quickly. When Ann and I reached our "seventies," we chose to have less responsibility and to travel a more leisurely pace in life. The Hale Realty office building on East Brainerd Road, including 2.4 acres of land, was sold for development. Change, once again, came our way as we no longer managed a staff and active real estate agents.

Ann and I continue in the real estate business under the Hale Realty banner. Managing investment and stock market funds occupies much of my time.

Life is good! Enjoy each day! Plan, Play, Pray and remember…

Yesterday is gone forever.
Today is the first day of the rest of your life…
And the best is yet to be.

A Salesman's Prayer

This is the beginning of a new day. God has given me this day to use as I will. I can waste it or use it for good. What I do today is important, because I'm exchanging a day of my life for it. When tomorrow comes, this day will be gone forever, leaving in its place something that I have traded for it. I want it to be gain, not loss; good, not evil; success, not failure, in order that I shall not regret the price I paid for it.

Amen

ATTITUDE FOR SUCCESS

The longer I live, the more I realize the impact of attitude on life.

Attitude, to me, is more important than facts. It is more important than the past, than education, than money, than circumstances, than failures, than successes, than what other people think or say or do. It is more important than appearance, giftedness or skill. It will make or break a company…a church…a home. The remarkable thing is we have a choice ever day regarding the attitude we will embrace for that day. We cannot change the inevitable. The only thing we can do is play on the one string we have, and that is our attitude…I am convinced that life is 10% what happens to me and 90% how I react to it. And so it is with you…

WE ARE IN CHARGE OF OUR ATTITUDES

A word from Bill McLaughlin

Raymond "Dub" Hale has been my mentor and friend for almost 60 years when we became acquaintances in a small town in West Tennessee.

In *It's A Long Way From Halls*, Raymond shares some of his life's experiences and stories.

His business career began as an entrepreneur in a small grocery store in Halls, Tennessee, that he started with borrowed money. After graduating from college and serving two years in the Air Force, he moved to Chattanooga, entered the real estate business, and enjoyed a successful sales and development career.

Having worked with him in both venues and living with his parents as a teenager, I came to associate myself as family. His disciplined work ethic through the years, together with his integrity, morals and Christian life has permitted him to have a very rewarding career.

Much of the success enjoyed in my own life is attributed to Raymond for his generosity, guidance and direction.

Bill McLaughlin
Senior Vice President
Real Estate Credit Officer, Retired
Union Planters Corporation
Memphis, Tennessee

To order copies of
It's a LONG WAY from HALLS

Please send check or money order to Raymond Hale
5 Talley Road, Chattanooga, Tennessee 37411
www.waldenhouse.com

Name _____

Shipping address _____

_____

City_____State_____Zip_____

Phone_____Email(optional)_____

Quantity _____ @ $29.95	=	$ _____	
Shipping first book @ $4.85	=	$ _____4.85	
Shipping additional books @ $3.00	=	$ _____	
TN residents add sales tax @9.725%	=	$ _____	
TOTAL	=	$ _____	

Thank you
for your order

Please send check or money order to: Raymond Hale,
5 Talley Road, Chattanooga, Tennessee 37411
www.waldenhouse.com

ITC Giovanni on Rose white opaque
Type and design by Karen Stone